THE GINGERBREAD AGE

The history of the Victorian Age

will never be written: we know

too much about it.

— LYTTON STRACHEY

THE GINGERBREAD AGE

A View of Victorian America by JOHN MAASS

BRAMHALL HOUSE, *New York*

Grateful acknowledgment is made to the following agents and publishers for permission to use material from their copyrighted works:

BRANDT & BRANDT, New York, N. Y., for permission to reprint a brief excerpt from THE MAGNIFICENT AMBERSONS, copyright, 1918, by Booth Tarkington.

HARPER & BROTHERS, New York, N. Y., for permission to reproduce two drawings from THE PASSPORT, by Saul Steinberg, copyright, 1954, by Saul Steinberg.

HOUGHTON MIFFLIN COMPANY, Boston, Mass., for permission to reprint a brief excerpt from the WPA VERMONT GUIDE, a volume in the AMERICAN GUIDE SERIES.

ALFRED A. KNOPF Incorporated, New York, N. Y., for permission to reprint a brief passage from THE HIGH WINDOW, by Raymond Chandler.

PENGUIN BOOKS LTD., Middlesex, England, for permission to use a quotation from THE THINGS WE SEE — INDOORS AND OUT, by Alan Jarvis.

RANDOM HOUSE, INC., New York, N. Y., for permission to reprint a selection from "A Rose for Emily" from THESE THIRTEEN, by William Faulkner, copyright, 1931, by William Faulkner.

RINEHART & COMPANY, INC., New York, N. Y., for permission to reprint a brief excerpt from GENERATION OF VIPERS, by Philip Wylie, copyright, 1942, by Philip Wylie.

THIS EDITION IS PUBLISHED BY BRAMHALL HOUSE,
A DIVISION OF CLARKSON N. POTTER, INC.,
BY ARRANGEMENT WITH HOLT, RINEHART & WINSTON, INC.

(E)

To Charles T. Coiner

Contents

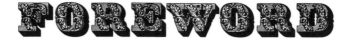

FOREWORD

Don't forget to speak scornfully
of the Victorian Age, there will
be time for meekness when you
try to better it.

— J. M. BARRIE

When I first came to this country I was startled by American nineteenth century buildings; though widely traveled I had never seen more fanciful houses. I began to sketch, paint and photograph them, then went to the libraries to learn more about these houses and their builders. There was little in print on the subject then and most of that was derogatory. Some books warned the reader to shut his eyes to one and all of these Victorian "monstrosities" lest his taste and morals be corrupted.

I hope this book will serve as an antidote to long-entrenched clichés.

It is not a work of formal scholarship. I have discovered no lost documents in archives or attics but have drawn freely on both nineteenth century sources and on the fast growing pile of research by present-day specialists on Americana. I am not an architectural historian and have avoided the intriguing vocabulary of that profession. There will be no further mention here of the trabeated versus arcuate systems of construction, machicolated stringcourses, splayed soffits, snecked rubble, sconcheons, riprap walls, calf's-tongue moldings, cusped voussoirs, counterlobed archivolts and twisted astragals.

You will find here the equivalent of almost two hundred thousand words by the "one picture is worth a thousand words" count. I have made a most determined effort to present visual evidence from many parts of the country but exact geographical balance cannot be achieved; there are over twenty thousand communities in the United States and most of them have some buildings of the period. You are invited to discover for yourself what's all around you.

This book is frankly biased in favor of an era whose spirit I like and admire. I am convinced that these striking landmarks of the vigorous Victorian past are more than just entertaining. Their boldness and vitality can teach a lesson to the conformist present.

CHAPTER 1

JUDGMENT UPON VICTORIAN

My nature is too passionate, my emotions are too fervent.

— QUEEN VICTORIA

The eighteen-year-old Princess Victoria became Queen in 1837. Styles of art and architecture have nothing at all to do with kings and queens; heralds proclaim the accession of a sovereign but they do not shout, "The Louis XV style is dead, long live the Louis XVI style!" The year 1837 merely happens to coincide with the gradual advent of a new kind of architecture; it was the architecture of the first industrial age and we call it Victorian*. Victoria lived on to 1901 but the last quarter century of her reign will not be discussed here; this book is about the period from 1837 to 1876, give or take a few years at either end.

Victorian architecture has long been in disrepute. Conventional architectural history ran something like this: A glorious procession of sharply defined styles from the ancient Egyptians, Babylonians, Assyrians, Greeks, Romans, onward and upward through the Middle Ages, Romanesque, Gothic, the Renaissance, the Georgian, the Greek Revival. Then the old-fashioned historian lapses into embarrassed silence, he mumbles about a sudden "disintegration of taste," "an age of horror" which lasts about half a century. From this abyss and degradation, American architecture is saved by a single genius. Some call him Henry Hobson Richardson, others give all the credit to Louis Sullivan, still others claim that Frank Lloyd Wright was the bold knight who slew the dragon of Victorianism. This melodrama has no basis in fact; it has now been discounted by scholars but hangs on as a popular and tenacious cliché. How did such a grotesque misconception become so firmly entrenched? Neither architecture nor posterity's judgment on it exists in a vacuum. We must view both against the background of their times.

For better or for worse, the period between 1840 and 1880 made America what it is today. The Civil War was such a traumatic event that it has somewhat overshadowed the many other dramatic develop-

* Non-English-speaking nations do not have this handy term because they lacked a convenient monarch.

ments of this era in our consciousness: At the outset, America was a largely agricultural country on the outer fringe of Western civilization — at the close, the United States was one of the great industrial powers of the world. The population tripled from seventeen to fifty million. Twelve states were admitted to the Union. In 1840 most travelers and goods still moved by coach, wagon and canalboat, there were only 2,800 miles of railroad track against 95,000 miles forty years later. The technological advances of this era are unmatched: The telegraph, the ocean steamer, modern machine tools, farm machinery, petroleum, photography, the sewing machine, the rotary printing press, gaslight, the electric motor, the telephone, electric lighting, all were invented or introduced during these forty years. The social changes were even more decisive — from this era date our present two party system, direct popular elections, our public school system, all our graduate schools, most scientific and professional societies, the first large corporations, mass immigration.

This was no mean age — in every field of human endeavor, the mid-nineteenth century was a time of frenetic activity and massive achievement. Is it reasonable to believe that during this entire period only incompetents and charlatans chose the ancient and honorable profession of architecture? Is it true that the generation which constructed the transatlantic cable and the transcontinental railroad was unable to build a decent house? The truth is that an enormously creative and progressive era produced an enormously creative and progressive architecture.

We have long condemned the buildings of this period because we disapproved of the people who built them.

> An age which could easily put up with the iniquity of drastic divisions between social classes, of extremes in wealth and poverty, which could pay fanatical attention to the humane treatment of domestic animals while tolerating inhuman slums and social brutality, must inevitably display the same muddle-headed values in its buildings . . . . As a spectacle both the architecture and the manners of the Victorians are merely comic, but seen in the social context their implications are tragic.*

* From Alan Jarvis's brilliant book *The Things We See — Indoors and Out.*

If the nineteenth century was the time of the sweatshop and the slum, it was also the time of reform and emancipation. This harsh judgment is one-sided, as one-sided as the popular image of Queen Victoria as a lifelong old prude who was never amused*.

The very word "Victorian" has now come to mean pompous, stuffy, prudish, hypocritical, narrow-minded. No man wants to be told, "Don't play the heavy Victorian father." No woman wants to be accused of taking a "Victorian attitude" towards the other sex. Victorian literature is guarded on the subject of sex; it was not considered a fit subject of conversation in mixed company. It would be most rash to draw from this any unfavorable conclusions about the Victorians' lovemaking.

As we have no personal experience with the Victorians of a century ago, we are heavily influenced by pictures. When we look at the great Brady photographs or perhaps at our own old family albums, we are struck by certain characteristics: These people are always dressed to the teeth, they pose stiffly against formal backgrounds of columns

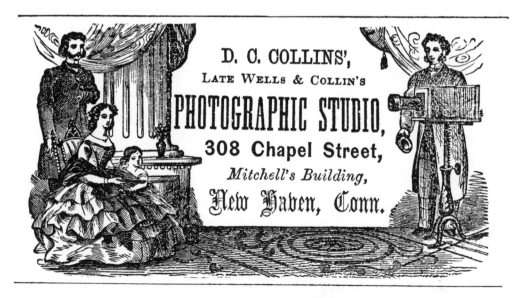

* Consider a few facts about the Queen which run counter to the accepted stereotype: Victoria fell in love with, proposed to and married a younger man; she often danced all night long; she was a tireless walker and horsewoman; a fresh air fiend who did not permit heated bedrooms; she liked her wine spiked with whisky; she sang in public and showed her art and needlework at public exhibitions; she published some of her diaries in book form; she revealed her innermost feelings and details of her private life in hundreds of frank letters to friends and relatives.

and drapery — and they never smile! This impression of crushing dignity is misleading. The Victorians could not smile for the camera because they had to hold still for exposures of several minutes; their heads were often clamped into an iron brace to insure rigidity.

As negative or currently unpopular characteristics of the Victorians have been so well publicized, we will stress here some of their impressive personal qualities. Nineteenth century Americans were not plagued by specialization or overspecialization. Every school child knows that Lincoln was in turn a farmhand, boatman, storekeeper, postmaster, surveyor, captain of militia, lawyer, state legislator and congressman. This kind of record was not at all unusual, most Americans — both men and women — up to Lincoln's time were Jacks-of-all-trades and masters of several. We are startled by the fact that Independence Hall was designed by a lawyer, the United States Capitol by a physician and the University of Virginia by an ex-President of the United States.

American Victorian architects often doubled as engineers, surveyors, draftsmen, railroad and canal builders, cabinetmakers, art teachers, illustrators and scene painters. They would not be able to obtain a license to practice architecture today; at least four years of specialized study at an accredited college are now required. The American Institute of Architects was founded in 1857 by thirteen men, its first president never went to college. The first school of architecture in the United States was established after the Civil War at the Massachusetts Institute of Technology; according to today's formalized standards there was not a single graduate architect in America until one Nathan Clifford Ricker got his diploma from the University of Illinois in 1873.

The work of these builders has been the target of much philistine criticism. Victorian houses are habitually labeled glum, grim, dark, dank, somber, sinister, forbidding, foreboding. At best, they are called uncomfortable. The charge of gloom is quite foolish — Victorian architecture is distinguished by its pleasurable fancy and exuberant color. The "dark" Victorian house had more and larger windows than earlier

American homes. It is true that these windows used to be barricaded with a fivefold layer of shutters, blinds, muslin curtains, velvet draperies and tasseled valances, but most of these are gone and light is flooding in.

We also know that the Victorians crammed and decorated their rooms in a way which is contrary to our designs for living. A floral carpet is underfoot and large-figured wallpaper all around; there are overstuffed chairs, tufted ottomans, marble-topped tables and carved sideboards; the remaining space is garnished with potted plants, bronzed statuary, plaster casts, wax flowers under glass domes, shell-work, beadwork, fringed cushions, gilt-framed pictures and petit-point mottoes; souvenirs and bric-a-brac are ranged on fretwork brackets and tiered whatnots. Stripped of this overgrowth, the Victorian parlor

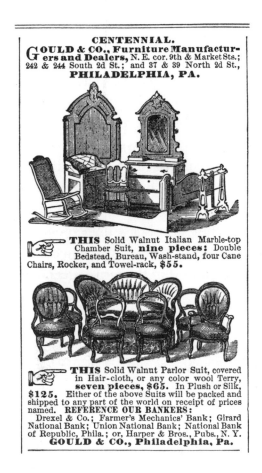

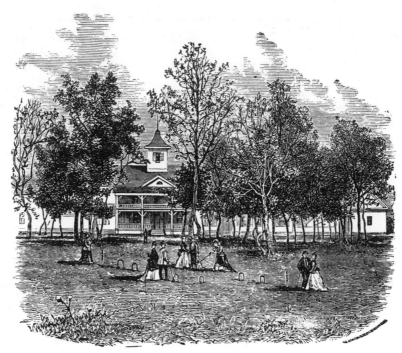

DELAWARE FARMER'S RESIDENCE.

with its parquet floor, high ceiling, tall windows, strong moldings and ample fireplace emerges as a very handsome room.

As for comfort, the so-called modern conveniences in heating, cooking, lighting and plumbing were all introduced during the nineteenth century.* European visitors were impressed by the convenience of American homes and "surprised at the lordly state of our citizens' style of living." These were the first houses to feature central heating by warm air furnaces, hot and cold running water, bathrooms, cooking ranges, indoor toilets. They also boast high rooms, a big kitchen, both a front and a back yard, ample storage space in cellar and attic — amenities which are not often found in the jerrybuilt homes of today.

In 1842 Andrew Jackson Downing wrote:

> In a country like ours where the population is comparatively sparse, civil rights equal and wages high, good servants and domestics are comparatively rare and not likely to retain their places for a long time. The maximum of comfort is therefore found in employing the smallest number of servants actually necessary. This may be greatly facilitated by introducing certain kinds of

* Air Conditioning is the only original contribution of the twentieth century.

12

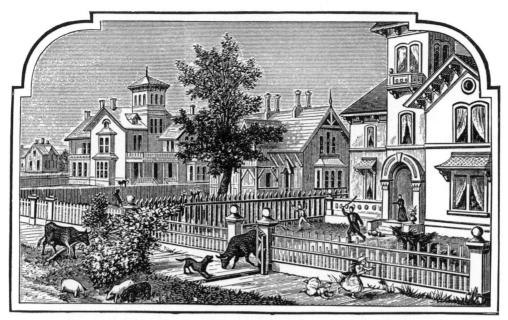

FIG. 22. PEOPLE WHO ARE TROUBLED BY THEIR NEIGHBORS.

The above illustration represents a common scene. The neighbors suspect each other, and they destroy the beauty of their grounds in the attempt to shut each other out. Suspicion and selfishness rule. Regardless of the rights of others, animals are allowed to trample to pieces the sidewalks, to destroy shade trees and to despoil the neighbor's yard. Inharmony, disorder, and ill-feeling among the people are characteristics of the neighborhood.

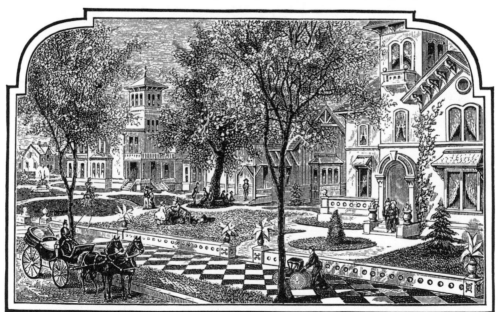

FIG. 23. THE NEIGHBORHOOD WHERE PEOPLE LIVE IN HARMONY.

This illustration represents a neighborhood where the people evidently do unto others as they wish others to do unto them. They trust each other. The barriers between them are removed. No animal is allowed to do injury. Enjoying peace and beauty they evidently desire that the neighbor shall share the same. This co-operation, kindness and regard for all, give the beauty, the harmony, the peace, and the evident contentment which are here presented.

13

domestic labor-saving apparatus to lessen the amount of services required or to render the performance easy. Among those which we would from experience especially recommend for cottages, are the rising cupboard or dumb-waiter, the speaking tube and the rotary pump.

The linking of high ideals and mechanical improvements is most characteristic; earnest, sincere moralizing is the very essence of Victorianism.

The Victorians regarded buildings as symbols and worked hard to make them "fitting." A bank building would display "strongly marked stability in harmony with the character of the institution," even a prison would be designed so that "the effect which it produces on the imagination of every passing spectator is peculiarly impressive, solemn and instructive."

Both large and small communities took great pride in a new public building; it would be described as "artistic," "a noble specimen of architecture," "an ornament to our fair city." This Victorian civic spirit presents an interesting contrast to our present brand of boosting which is only concerned with size (NEW 5,000-SEAT MUNICIPAL AUDITORIUM) and cost (NEW THREE MILLION DOLLAR HIGH SCHOOL).

Tastes and prejudices, fads and fashions come and go. There is superior and inferior work within each generation but there are of course no "good" and "bad" periods of design. It is a truism to state that architecture is an expression of its time. Victorian buildings are perfect symbols of an era which was not given to understatement. They are in complete harmony with the heavy meals, strong drink, elaborate clothes, ornate furnishings, flamboyant art, melodramatic plays, loud music, flowery speeches and thundering sermons of mid-nineteenth century America.

Most of our own buildings stand on the shifting quicksand of insecurity — Victorian architecture was founded on the rock of superb confidence.

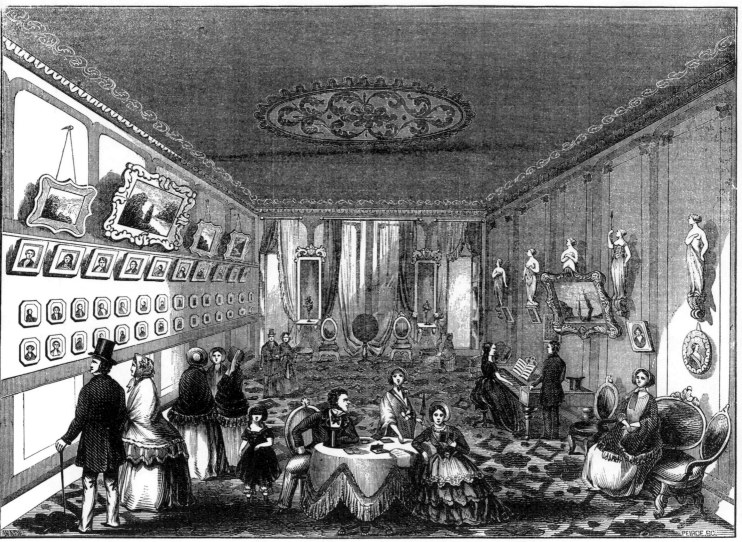

BALL'S GREAT DAGUERRIAN GALLERY OF THE WEST.

This elegant interior of the eighteen fifties is a photographer's studio in Cincinnati, Ohio. It was not only decorated with 187 specimens of Mr. Ball's art but with paintings and statues of the Goddesses of Poesy, Music, Science, Purity, Religion and Beauty as well. "Every piece of furniture in this gallery is a master-piece of mechanical and artistic skill. The very seat on which you sit and the carpet on which you tread seem to be a gem culled from the fragrant lap of Flora."

17

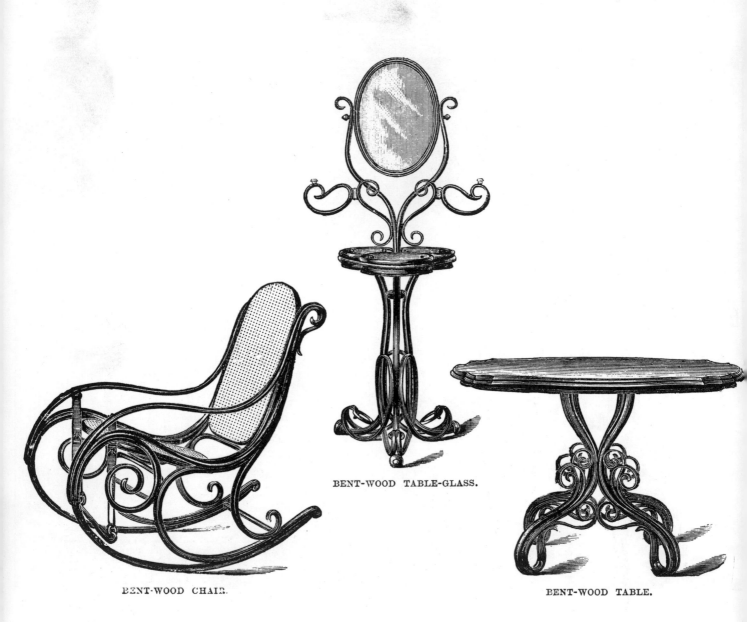

BENT-WOOD TABLE-GLASS.

BENT-WOOD CHAIR.

BENT-WOOD TABLE.

The masterpieces of Victorian design — Thonet's bentwood furniture. These exuberant forms grew out of a process invented by Michael Thonet: bending wood under steam heat. Thonet's factories in Austria exported to all parts of the world. One strong and graceful type of chair proved so popular that more than fifty million were sold.

18

Hints to the Host and Hostess.

Take the baggage-checks, and give personal attention to having the trunks conveyed to your residence, relieving the guest of all care in the matter.

Having received intelligence of the expected arrival of a guest, if possible have a carriage at the depot to meet the friend. Various members of the family being with the carriage will make the welcome more pleasant.

Have a warm, pleasant room especially prepared for the guest, the dressing-table being supplied with water, soap, towel, comb, hair-brush, brush-broom, hat-brush, pomade, cologne, matches, needles and pins. The wardrobe should be conveniently arranged for the reception of wearing apparel. The bed should be supplied with plenty of clothing, a side-table should contain writing materials, and the center-table should be furnished with a variety of entertaining reading matter.

Arrange to give as much time as possible to the comfort of the guest, visiting places of amusement and interest in the vicinity. This should all be done without apparent effort on your part. Let your friends feel that the visit is a source of real enjoyment to you; that through their presence and company you have the pleasure of amusements and recreation that would, perhaps, not have been enjoyed had they not come. Treat them with such kindness as you would like to have bestowed upon yourself under similar circumstances.

At the close of their stay, if you would be happy to have the visitors remain longer, you will frankly tell them so. If they insist upon going, you will aid them in every way possible in their departure. See that their baggage is promptly conveyed to the train. Examine the rooms to find whether they have forgotten any article that they would wish to take. Prepare a lunch for them to partake of on their journey. Go with them to the depot. Treat them with such kindness and cordiality to the close that the recollection of their visit will ever be a bright spot in their memory. Remain with them until the train arrives. They would be very lonely waiting without you. You will ever remember with pleasure the fact that you made the last hours of their visit pleasant. And thus, with the last hand-shaking, and the last waving of adieu, as the train speeds away, keep up the warmth of hospitality with your guests to the very end. It is, perhaps, the last time you will ever see them.

What was it like to be a guest in a Victorian home?
Hill's Manual, a highly popular book of etiquette, tells all. The last sentence is characteristically Victorian.

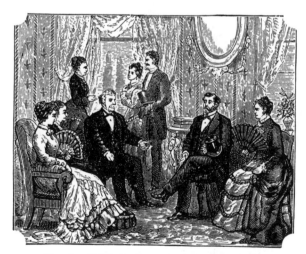

FIG. 7. GENTILITY IN THE PARLOR.

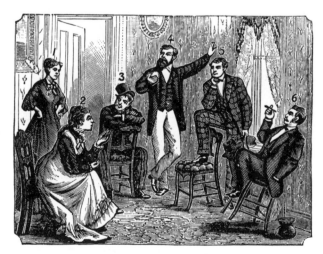

FIG. 6. UNGRACEFUL POSITIONS.

The figures in the above illustration represent graceful postures to be assumed by both ladies and gentlemen in the parlor. As will be seen, whether holding hat or fan, either sitting or standing, the positions are all easy and graceful.

To assume an easy genteel attitude, the individual must be self-possessed. To be so, attention must be given to easy flow of language, happy expression of thought, study of cultured society and the general laws of etiquette.

No. 1. Stands with arms akimbo.
" 2. Sits with elbows on the knees.
" 3. Sits astride the chair, and wears his hat in the parlor.
" 4. Stains the wall paper by pressing against it with his hand; eats an apple alone, and stands with his legs crossed.
No. 5. Rests his foot upon the chair-cushion.
" 6. Tips back his chair, soils the wall by resting his head against it, and smokes in the presence of ladies.

19

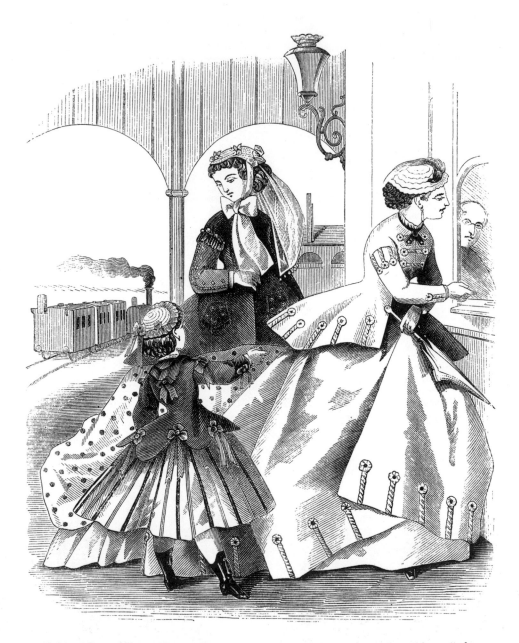

Left-hand Figure. WALKING TOILET.—The Pamela bonnet is of straw, ornamented with small bouquets of rose-buds; a long tulle or crape veil falls behind; pink ribbon strings. The pardessus is made of black silk, the trimming consisting of guipure and jet buttons disposed down the fronts and sleeves. The dress is of a lilac light fancy silk. It is worn with a petticoat trimmed at the bottom with a large plaited flounce.

Right-hand Figure. TRAVELLING TOILET.—The Lamballe hat is of fancy straw, and has on the front a bird with a long tail. The dress, pardessus, and skirt are made of gray poplin, and simply ornamented all round with gimp cord, disposed at equal distances, as clearly shown in our illustration.

COSTUME FOR A LITTLE GIRL.—The round straw hat is trimmed round the brim with a ruche of blue silk, and a bow behind with two short ends. The pardessus is made of blue silk, with a hood, and ornamented with bows of ribbon. Plain skirt of a striped fancy material.

Architecture and the design of clothes are inseparable. To understand either subject, you must study both.

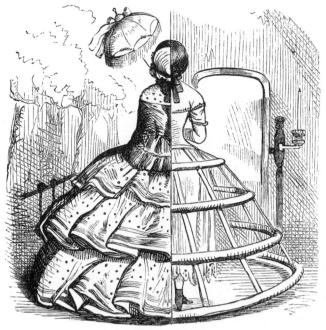

DRESS AND THE LADY.

The Victorian woman was usually well covered, but on festive occasions the ladies appeared in some of the most revealing gowns known to Western civilization. The effect must have been devastating.

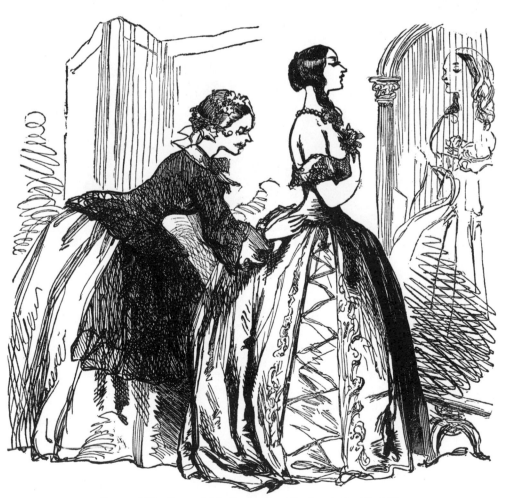

LADY. "Don't you think the Dress *rather* low in the Neck?"
DRESSMAKER. Oh! no, ma'am: only *Dressy*."

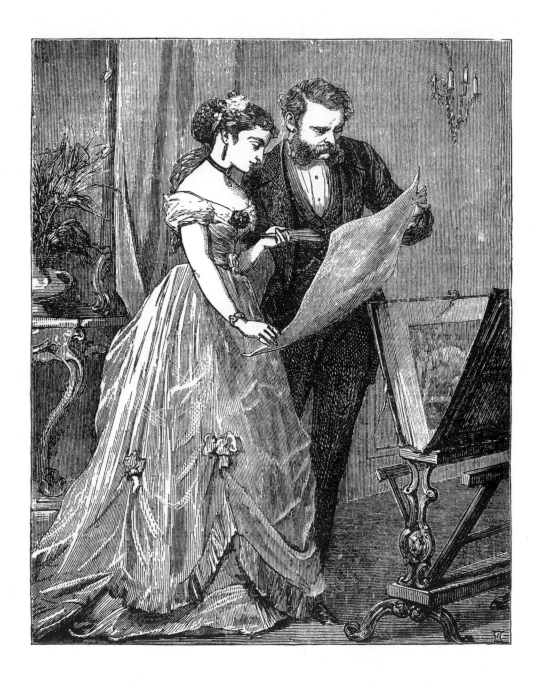

The nineteenth century regarded both buildings and clothes as symbols. Victorian fashions were most artfully designed to accentuate the difference between the sexes. The male is made to look bold and strutting, the female languishing and curvaceous.

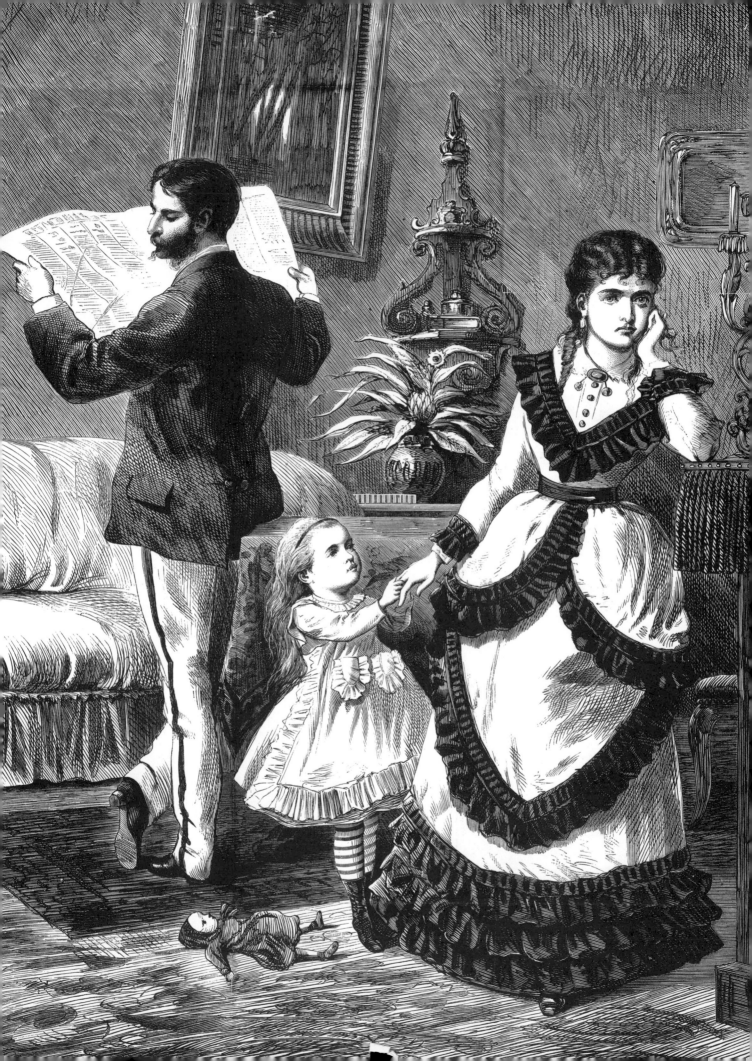

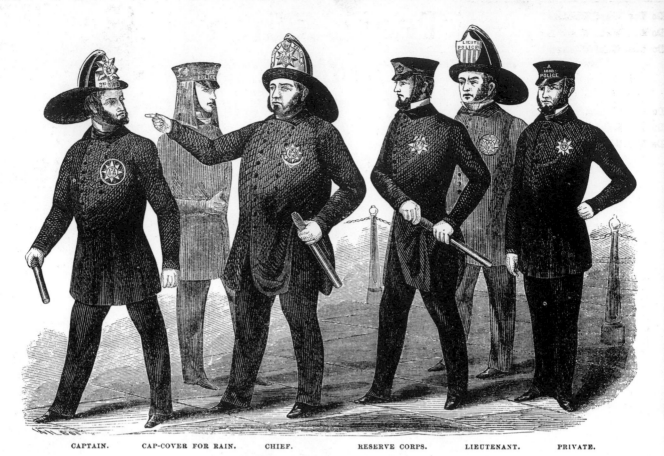

CAPTAIN.   CAP-COVER FOR RAIN.   CHIEF.   RESERVE CORPS.   LIEUTENANT.   PRIVATE.

NEW REGULATION UNIFORM OF THE NEW YORK POLICE.

Victorian fashions show great inventiveness in design; the fashion plates also display characteristic masculine and feminine attitudes and gestures.

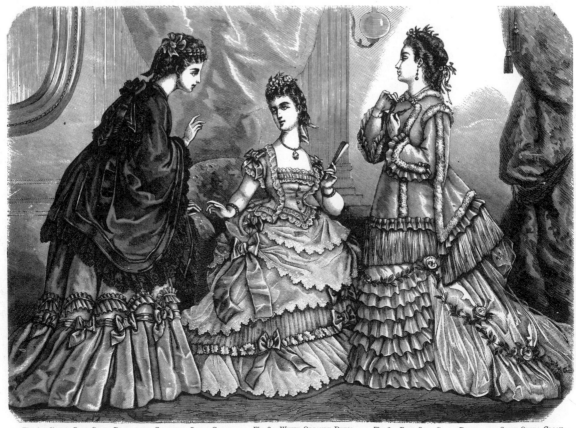

Fig. 1.—PEARL GROS GRAIN DRESS WITH CASHMERE OPERA CLOAK.   Fig. 2.—WHITE ORGANDY DRESS.   Fig. 3.—BLUE SILK GAUZE DRESS WITH SATIN OPERA CLOAK.

LADIES' RECEPTION DRESSES.

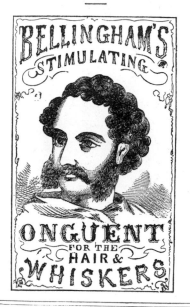
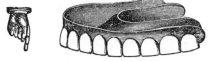
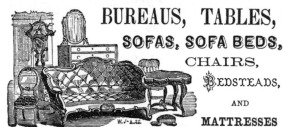
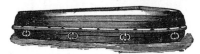
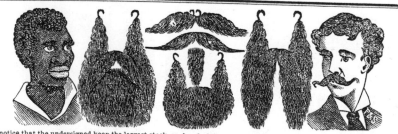

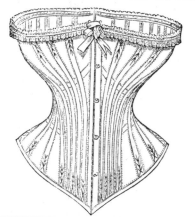
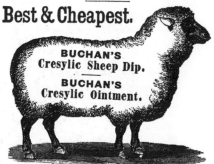
Nineteenth century advertisements are most revealing.

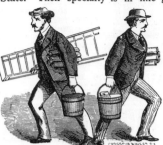 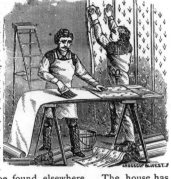
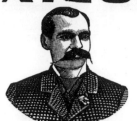
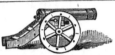
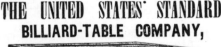
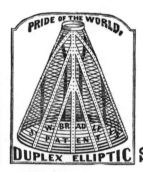
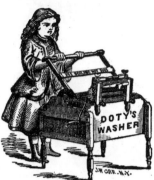
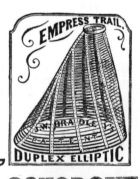
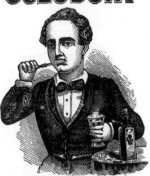
Both words and images have the vivid qualities of directness and overstatement.

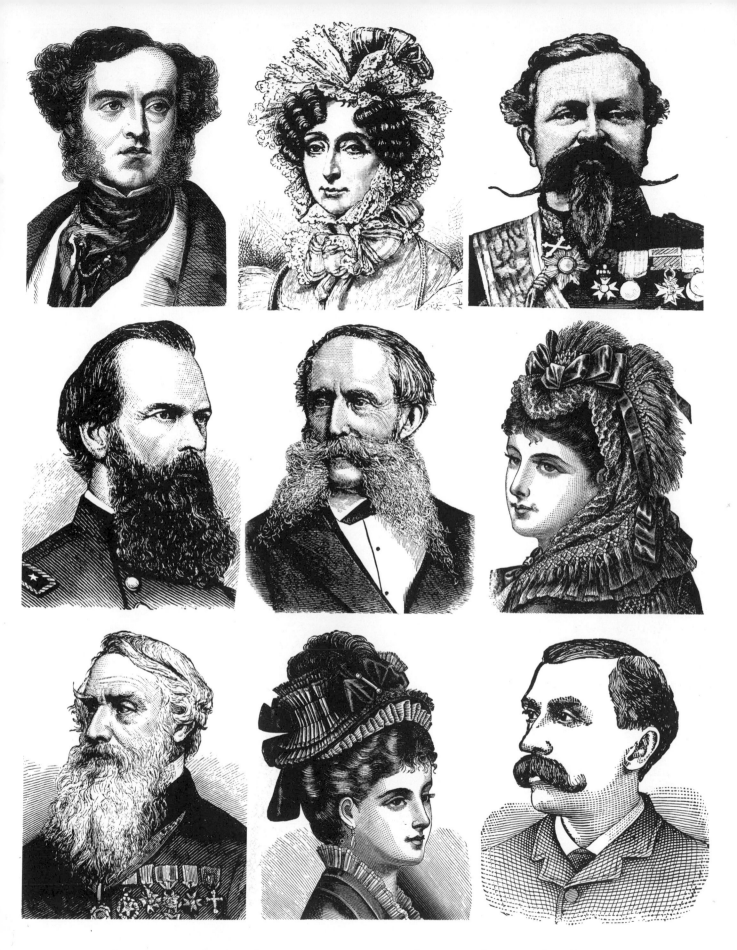

The Victorians displayed striking imagination in designing their own heads.

CHAPTER 2

A WORLD OF STYLES

*The Styles of Louis XIV, XV, XVI
or Gothic are to Architecture what
a feather is on a woman's head; it
is sometimes pretty, though not
always and never anything more.*

— LE CORBUSIER

The ancient Romans wrote on wax tablets with a pointed tool, the *stilus*. From this we get our word "style" via the meaning of "writing" and "manner of expression characteristic of a writer." From literature the term spread to art, to architecture and finally to clothes. The word should really be spelled "stile"; the Y crept in by confusion with the Greek word *stylos* which means column.

This was an easy mistake to make; as the nineteenth century opened, every stylish new building sported a portico of Grecian columns. What we call the Greek Revival in the United States was part of a truly international style. (It is usually called Regency style in Britain, Empire or Classicism on the European continent.) Marble halls rose in every great city of Europe from Dublin to St. Petersburg; no matter whether church or palace, stock exchange or shipyard, they all appeared in Grecian dress. So did fashionable ladies for a few giddy

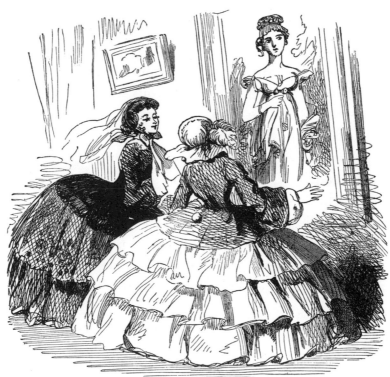

"ARABELLA MARIA. "Only to think, Julia dear, that our Mothers wore such ridiculous fashions as these!"
BOTH. "Ha! ha! ha! ha!"

31

years; even in the United States these "scanty, indecent" Greek style gowns were seen, "worn with the fewest possible underclothes, a fashion both abominably ugly and very unhealthy" writes a critic in the well-corseted eighteen sixties.

American Grecian buildings rank with the finest of the Old World. Only the United States planned and built its capital city during this period and no other country ever had an architect for a chief of state. Thomas Jefferson was a great designer and a most ardent advocate for the Greek Revival. Early Washington bears the imprint of Jefferson's good taste and good sense*.

The Greek Revival actually struck deeper roots in the United States than it did in Europe. There it was mainly applied to great ceremonial buildings and aristocratic mansions; over here "the country was studded with 'temples' from court houses down to bird boxes. Every carpenter ploughed, tongued and grooved the Antique into cornices, with triglyphs, modules, consoles and the like." We have been taught to regard "Greek" and "beautiful" as one and the same and the Greek Revival in America has left a treasure of beauty. There are no lovelier houses anywhere than the grand plantations of Louisiana ringed with tall wooden columns. Shaded Main Street in Nantucket town with its white Grecian homes must be one of the most beautiful streets in the world. Slavery built the one and the odorous whaling trade the other, which goes to show that we must keep our moral sense and our taste for beauty in separate compartments.

The Victorians, of course, moralized on every possible occasion and they attacked the Greek style upon moral grounds. Actually, the Greek Revival had run its course in the forties because it was no longer adequate. This beautiful, serene style is essentially an architecture of façades. Fenestration was always a problem in a porticoed building; even such a lover of the antique as Goethe had recognized that "columns and windows are a contradiction." The Greek temples

---

* Jefferson would be horrified by the huge, "Neo-Greek" buildings of twentieth century Washington which so closely resemble Hitler's Berlin chancellery and Stalin's Moscow subway.

had of course been windowless and the dwellings of the ancient Greeks and Romans were without columns. The ground plan of a Greek Revival building had to conform to the symmetrical elevation. This could be made to work in formal designs like royal palaces, state capitols and even town halls but it was a straitjacket for builders who were called upon to solve the everyday problems of an increasingly complex industrial civilization.

The keenest critic of the Greek mode was Horatio Greenough who called himself a Yankee stonecutter. Here is his comment on the United States Mint at Philadelphia:

> A showy front masks all these things and adorns Chestnut Street by the maimed quotation of a passage of Greek eloquence relating to something else. A large brick chimney rising in the rear talks English and warns you that the façade is to be taken with some grains of allowance.

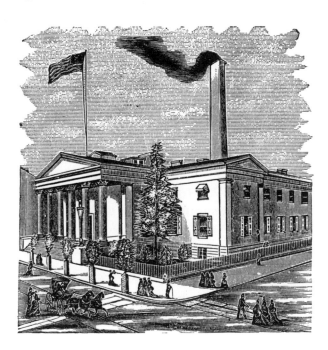

At the New Orleans Mint, even the chimney in the back yard "talked Greek"; it was built in the shape of a huge column!

It is odd that Greenough did not himself practice what he

preached. In 1832, Congress commissioned him to carve a marble statue of George Washington and Greenough set to work in Florence to fashion his masterpiece:

> It is the birth of my thought and I have sacrificed to it the flower of my days and the freshness of my strength, its every lineament has been moistened with the sweat of my toil and the tears of my exile.

It proved to be an ill-fated work. While being hoisted aboard ship, the colossal sculpture slipped and plunged into the Tyrrhenian Sea. Salvaged from the harbor bottom, it was at long last unveiled in 1842. Few works of art have met with such a unanimous reception, Congress, critics and plain citizens alike were horrified — Greenough had represented the Father of Our Country as a seminude Greek god! The shocking statue lingered on the Capitol grounds for some years and was finally put away in the Smithsonian Institution. There it still sits — a monument to the decline and fall of the Greek Revival in America.

Gervase Wheeler, the accomplished author of *Rural Homes* or *Sketches of Houses Suited to American Country Living* marshaled the following Romantic argument against the Greek style:

> Nestling among the trees not far from the church should be seen the oft-alluded-to school house, low, rustic and shaded. A distinct porch and yard for boys and girls and above the roof a little bell cot. No columns, nor pediment, nor classic pretension; the village children make not the dead languages of Greece and Rome their study, why surround them with their architecture? Let me plead for a flower garden attached to the school house — beautiful lessons of industry and love and reverence can be taught by flower culture.

Samuel Sloan, that most characteristic Victorian architect who was busy with both pen and T-square, made the unkindest attack upon the Greek Revival:

> In passing a fine residence, the location of which we need not name, a friend inquired whether it was a church, college or court house, which we were not able to answer until we ap-

proached close enough to determine by the drapery in the window that it was a dwelling house. It was a classic building and a fine specimen of architecture, but was it domestic architecture? Without doubt the gentlemanly proprietor of the classic house above spoken of, would have scorned to receive from the painter's hand the picture of Apollo as his own portrait, and yet he has permitted his architect to disguise under the semblance of a heathen temple, the real character of his place of residence.

The crack about the "heathen temple" was a devastating argument in those days although hundreds of churches had been built in the un-Christian Greek style. When the Greek Revival went out of fashion, the Victorians pretended that it had been immoral all along.

What was to take the place of the outmoded Greek manner? It had to be some other style with a past. A Victorian gentleman would not appear in public hatless and shirtsleeved. In the same way, the bare bones of every proper building had to be clothed in outer garments of "historical" design. While the nineteenth century was plunging ahead to triumphs of science, industry and social progress, it kept resolutely looking backwards in matters of literature and art. The Victorians adored The Far Away and The Long Ago. Their writing and painting is all intertwined with history and geography. The giants of Romantic literature — Byron, Scott, Irving, Hawthorne, Longfellow — all took their subject matter from the past and often wrote straight history as well. Popular novels and periodicals followed suit. The fine arts also bore down heavily on the romance of yesteryear, both costumed and undraped. Victorian morality frowned upon nudity in a painting or sculpture, but it could be made respectable by labeling such a daring work of art "Eve" or "Adriadne." Only the well-to-do could afford oil paintings in gold frames but plenty of art was well within the means of the average family. The middle class home was amply stocked with steel engravings and lithographs, some on the walls and more in albums, scrapbooks and "parlor companions" which were piled on tables. Children, gentlemen callers and female visitors were always leafing through these big picture books, scenes of chivalry and olden times abounded and as all well-brought-up females dabbled

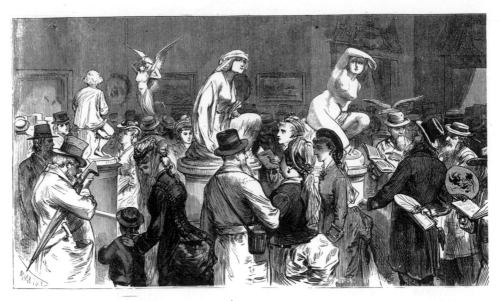

in art, they sketched these pretty conceits in water color or reproduced them in needlework. Such were the literary and artistic wellsprings of Romantic architecture.

Homeowners and local builders drew their ideas of stylish design from the so-called pattern books. These guides were themselves patterned after English books of this type. They usually open with some general and moralizing observations on the art of architecture and the pleasures of home. The main body of the book presents detailed descriptions of individual houses, well illustrated by wood-engraved plans and views. Some were actual houses built by the designer-author, others remained paper projects forever. A few random chapters on such subjects as heating, ventilating, joinery, furniture and landscape gardening bring up the rear. Cost estimates are often given. The high purchasing power of a dollar a hundred years ago is quite startling to us — "a snug, little model cottage for a workman" with six rooms on two floors could be built for "a trifle over $300"! The pattern books filled a real need at a time when there were few trained designers and no architectural magazines in the United States. They have never disappeared from the American scene. Pattern books for "Cape Cod Cottages" and "California Ranch Houses" are big sellers today.

Most of the houses in pattern books are labeled with the names of styles. An 1841 English book by Richard Brown is the ultimate in this respect. It features such delightful follies as "Pompeian Suburban

DESIGN XV.

A Cottage for a Mechanic or Clerk.

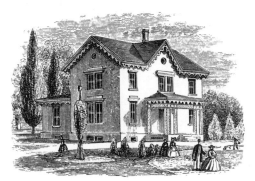

FIG. 64.

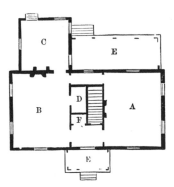

FIG. 65.—PRINCIPAL FLOOR.

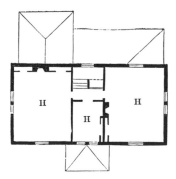

FIG. 66.—SECOND FLOOR.   (148)

Villa," "Venetian Summer Residence," "Lancastrian Embattled Mansion," "Persian Pavilion," "Chinese Casino" and "Palatial Building in the Morisco-Spanish Style." Not one of these was ever built but Hafod on the Welsh river Ystwyth with its Gothic conservatory, Mogul library and Italian campanile is an actual country house in this romantic spirit.

American pattern books present many ingenious arguments in favor of their "Gothic Cottages" and "Tuscan Villas."

Not a little of the delight of beautiful buildings for a cultivated mind grows out of the SENTIMENT of architecture, or the association connected with certain styles.

So an English home suggests "Merry England, hearty hospitality, joyous old sports, romance and chivalry," an Italian villa "may recall the classic beauty of that fair and smiling land."

However the reader is warned against the following procedure:

If the gentleman or lady about to build possess at all a literary or even only a picture-book-loving taste, some "Architectural Design Book for the Million" has been turned over, and, after many tea-table discussions upon the merits of the "Swiss Cottage Style," the "Anglo-Norman," the "Etruscan" or the "Castellated Gothic," some pretty picture house has been selected. Armed with that, an architect from the city has been called upon, the picture shown to him, the groundplan of the house determined, and, finally a "set of drawings" engaged to be furnished by a certain day, and at a stipulated price.

Gervase Wheeler, the author of this passage, pointed out that

an architect who has the interests of his noble science at heart will ALWAYS insist on studying the site and the tastes or habits of life of the future occupants.

He gave this sensible advice in 1854, fifteen years before Frank Lloyd Wright was even born.

The dazzling and somewhat confusing panorama of Victorian styles has been miscalled "The Battle of Styles" from the hindsight of later critics. Actually, there was no battle but peaceful coexistence of many styles. The most accomplished Victorian architects worked in the greatest variety of styles: The Parisian halls of Vassar College, the belfries of the Smithsonian, the Gothic spires of New York's Grace Episcopal Church and Roman Catholic St. Patrick's Cathedral were all designed by the same man, James Renwick, Jr., within a few years. Leopold Eidlitz, who was a graduate of the Vienna Polytechnic and had more academic training than native-born American builders, would erect a Swiss chalet, a Romanesque church or a Saracenic* villa at short notice.

Because the nineteenth century paraded such a panoply of architectural styles many people still believe that the Victorians were mere imitators. *The charge is false.* Instead of clinging to traditional rules and academic schemes, the Victorian builders attacked each new problem in a spirit of vigorous experimentation. Even their gallant failures have the merit of individuality. Their styles were only convenient labels to make new designs more salable and please the clients' cultural aspirations. The historicizing flummery usually covered a very sound body. In any case, close copying was physically impossible for nineteenth century American builders, very few of whom had traveled abroad or had access to architectural reference libraries.

The deliberate imitating of alien and defunct architectural styles belongs to a later era. It began in the eighteen nineties when American architecture sank beneath the pall of the so-called Beaux Arts system. This studied nonsense dominated architectural training in the United States until about the time of World War II. The old Madison Square Garden, for example, featured a replica of the Giralda of Seville which happens to be a Moorish minaret disguised as a cathedral bell tower. New York's Pennsylvania Railroad Station (A.D. 1910) is patterned after the Baths of the Roman emperor Caracalla (A.D. 186 to 217). These buildings were designed by the celebrated firm of Charles Follen McKim, William Rutherford Mead and Stanford White, the best of the Beaux Arts crowd. Their competitors cluttered every American city

* He designed P. T. Barnum's Iranistan at Bridgeport, Connecticut. The showman invited a thousand guests to the housewarming and kept an elephant on the grounds; Barnum's Oriental villa burned down in 1858.

with cheapjack imitations. It is therefore possible to take a vicarious architectural trip around the world in eighty minutes in most large American cities. This is not an edifying journey — people who are incessantly exposed to false standards lose the ability to distinguish true values.

Your local high school is probably an inflated caricature of a medieval college where basketball is played in a spurious Gothic hall. That forged Roman temple on your Main Street is where the president of the Second National Bank officiates as high priest. Some of the best families in your community are likely to own "Tudor" residences; this means that they live in stucco houses with dummy beams appliquéd on top to imitate the look of a fifteenth century English cottage. The most convenient period to steal ideas from is the American past: phony "Georgian" and "colonial" buildings are everywhere. Both your drive-in ice cream parlor and your undertaker's parlor may be counterfeits of Independence Hall or Mount Vernon.

Mumford has put the blame where it belongs:

> Architecture, like government, is about as good as a community deserves. The shell which we create for ourselves marks our spiritual development as plainly as that of a snail denotes its species.

All this gross and degrading fakery has been going on in *your* home town and lifetime. Calling the Victorians imitators is to attribute our own sins to a more upright generation.

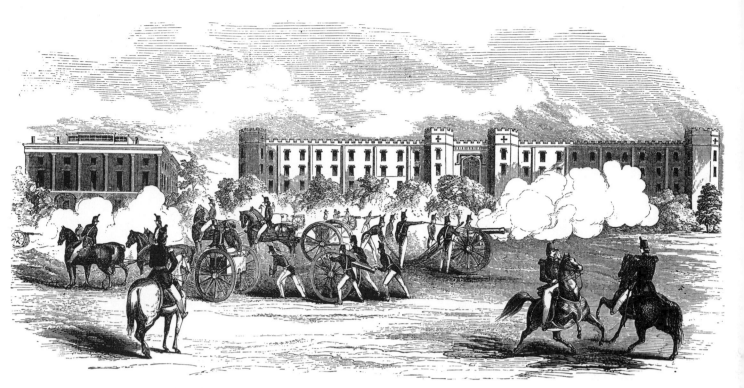

VIEW OF THE U. S. MILITARY ACADEMY AND THE NEW BARRACKS, AT WEST POINT, N. Y.

The "Castellated" or "Embattled" style was considered especially fitting for buildings of martial character like military schools and armories.

THE EASTERN PENITENTIARY.

NEW COUNTY PRISON.

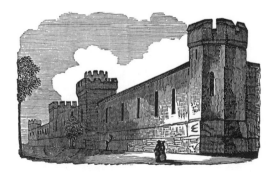
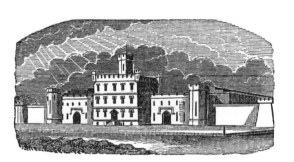

Most Victorian prisons were made to look like medieval fortresses. Both these examples are in Philadelphia and still in use. The County Prison was described as follows: "At a distance one might suppose it was some baronial castle of the olden time, suddenly transported, by some magic incantation, from the distant shores of Europe." It also boasts a debtors' wing in the Egyptian style, a cruel and unusual form of punishment which was inflicted on the convicts of several states in the thirties and forties.

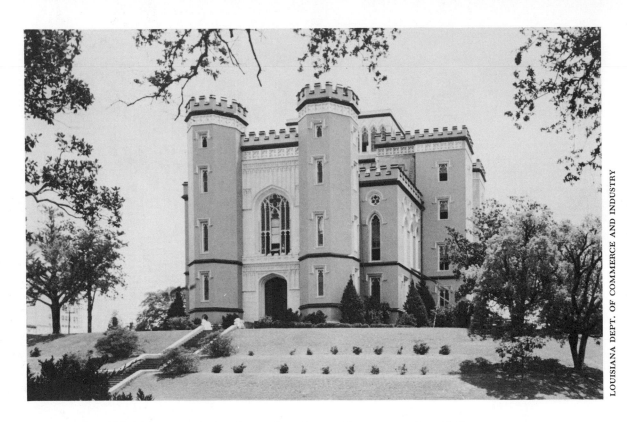

The Old Louisiana State Capitol at Baton Rouge is a fanciful structure; inside is a fantastic Gothic dome of iron and stained glass. Mark Twain did not like it at all . . . "a whitewashed castle, with turrets and things, materials all ungenuine within and without, pretending to be what they are not," and he knew exactly where this sort of thing came from: "Sir Walter Scott is probably responsible for the Capitol Buildings, for it is not conceivable that this little sham castle would ever have been built if he had not run the people mad, a couple of generations ago, with his medieval romances."

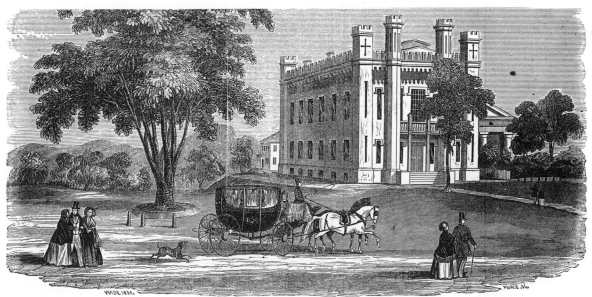

VIEW OF THE TOWN HALL, NORTHAMPTON, MASSACHUSETTS.

This castlelike town hall dates from 1851. The Greek temple on the right is the Unitarian church.

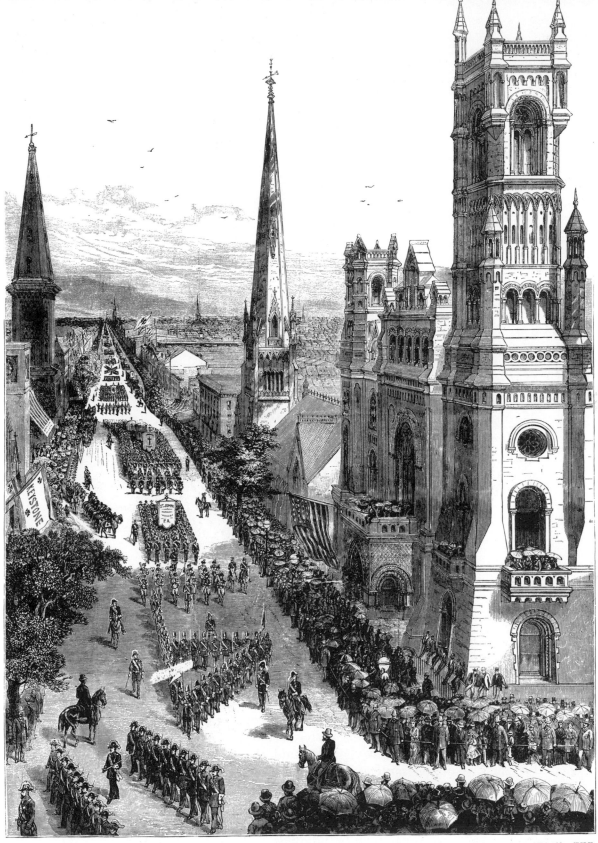

VISIT OF THE GRAND COMMANDERY OF THE UNITED STATES KNIGHTS TEMPLARS TO THE EXPOSITION—THE COLUMN PASSING THE MASONIC TEMPLE IN BROAD STREET, PHILADELPHIA.

The looming castle in the foreground is a Masonic temple. The interior boasts a Corinthian staircase, an Italian Renaissance library, an Egyptian Hall, a Moorish Hall and a Gothic Hall!

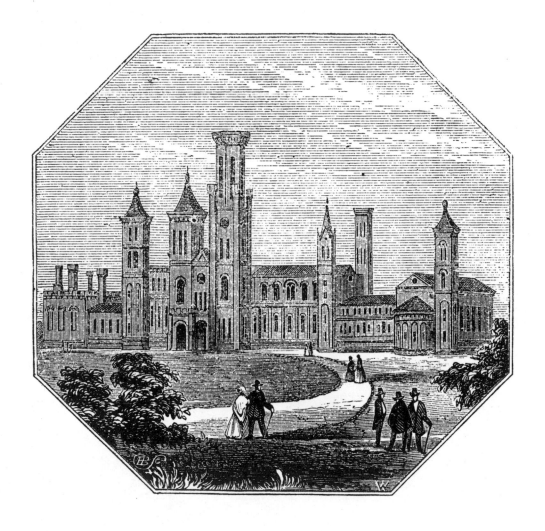

The origin of the Smithsonian Institution is most romantic — the illegitimate son of an English duke left his fortune to a country he had never seen — and it is appropriately housed in a masterpiece of romantic architecture. It was begun in 1847 and took six years to build; the Smithsonian was declared to be "the first unecclesiastical edifice of this architectural order ever erected in this country"; its style was variously described as "Norman," "Lombard" or "Byzantine." The many-towered Smithsonian castle of red sandstone is a striking sight from every direction and a much more interesting structure than Washington's many white buildings in bogus Greek style.

44

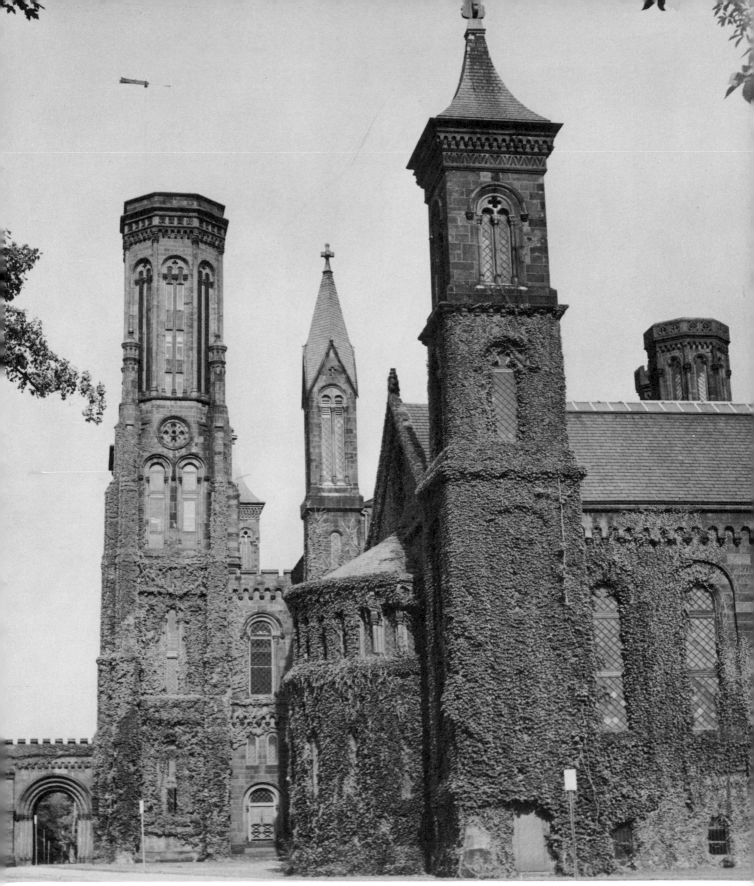

45

The Chicago Water Tower looks like a giant toy and is a well-loved landmark of the Windy City. It was built in the sixties and survived the Great Fire of 1871.

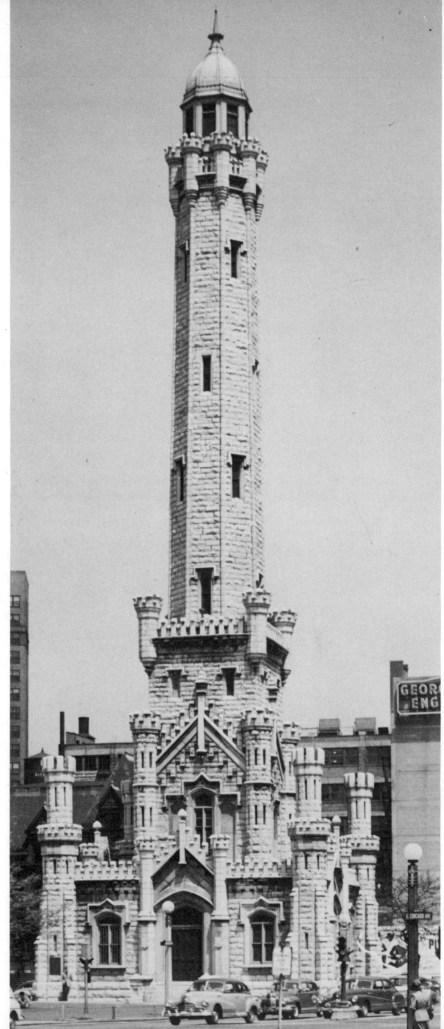

Few Americans built castles to live in during the early Victorian period — perhaps it was considered ill fitting for the citizen of a republic to dwell in feudal style. Some very pretentious castles were put up by the brash merchant princes of a later era. Biltmore, the gigantic Vanderbilt chateau near Asheville, North Carolina; Boldt's Castle, a hotel tycoon's unfinished residence on the Saint Lawrence River and Bannerman's Castle, an arms dealer's island fortress in the Hudson, all date from the heyday of the *nouveaux riches* around the turn of the twentieth century.

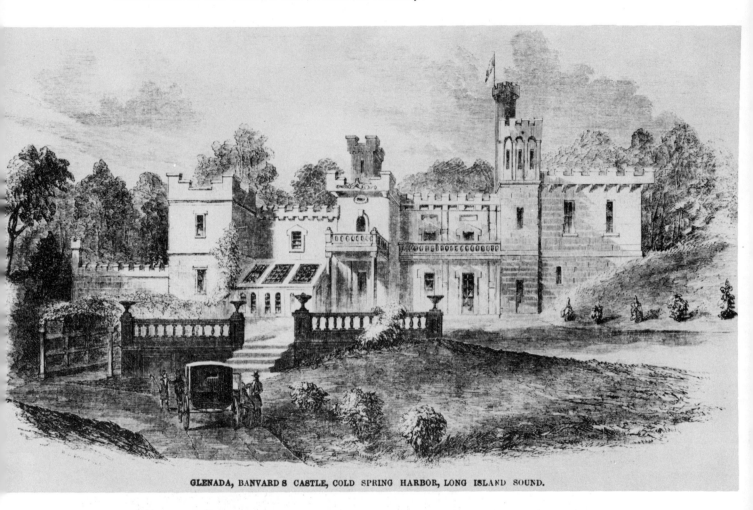

GLENADA, BANVARD'S CASTLE, COLD SPRING HARBOR, LONG ISLAND SOUND.

Banvard's Castle was an "Italian Castellated Villa" in "a lovely and romantic glen." Banvard is now forgotten but was a colorful celebrity in the forties and fifties. He painted the largest picture in the world — a "Panorama of the Mississippi"; it was claimed to be three miles long and displayed on two revolving cylinders to great crowds. He also wrote dramas, travel books and thousands of poems. In his old age Banvard went West and died in South Dakota.

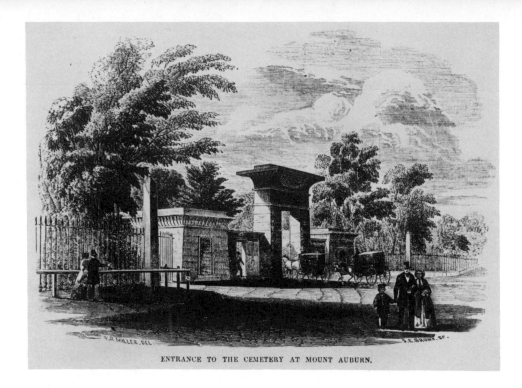

ENTRANCE TO THE CEMETERY AT MOUNT AUBURN.

Bonaparte's Egyptian expedition was a military and political fiasco but it brought the mysterious art of ancient Egypt to the attention of a fascinated West. Although the architecture of Egypt is so far removed in both time and space, dozens of "Egyptian Revival" buildings were erected in the United States. Because of the ancient Egyptians' preoccupation with the afterlife, their style was deemed particularly suitable for cemetery architecture. Boston's Mount Auburn Cemetery is a famous example.

The massive character of Egyptian architecture also recommended it to prison builders. This curious engraving shows New York's City Jail, nicknamed "The Tombs." It was demolished in the nineties.

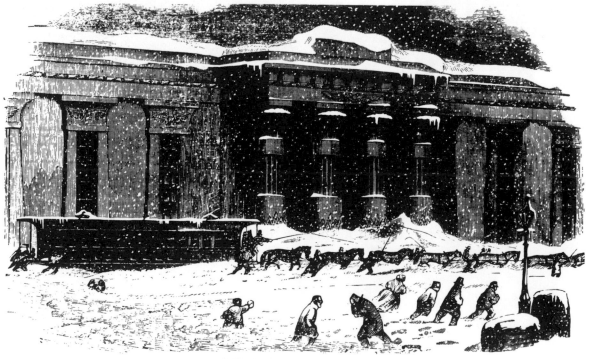

SCENE IN CENTRE STREET, NEW YORK CITY, DURING THE LATE SNOW STORM.

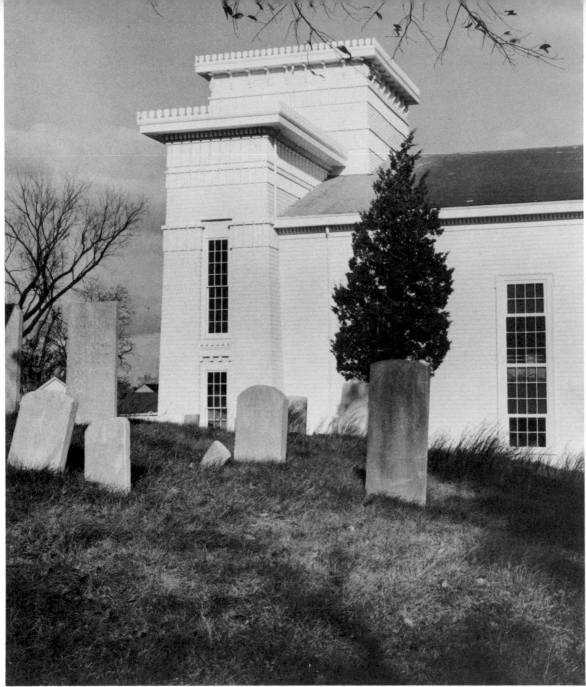

The most charming specimen of Americanized Egyptian is the Whalers Presbyterian Church at Sag Harbor, New York. It was designed by the self-taught architect Minard Lafever and built by ship's carpenters in the forties. The white, clapboarded building looks quite at home in its Long Island setting though it has some strange details: The walls are "battered" or sloping in the manner of ancient temples on the Nile; the parapets are decorated with rows of whalers' blubber spades. A tall steeple, shaped like a mariner's spyglass, was blown down by a hurricane in 1938.

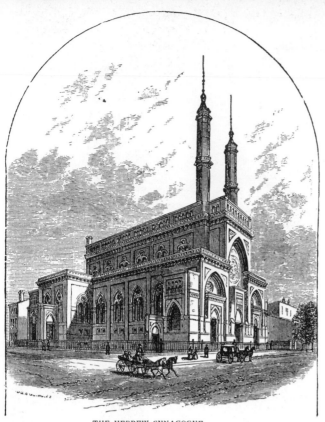

THE HEBREW SYNAGOGUE.

The proper Victorians read the oriental tales of wicked Lord Byron and wicked Richard Burton with shudders of delight. Numerous Victorian-Oriental buildings in the United States testify to the fascination of the glamorous East.

The Victorian Age developed some scruples as to whether it was fitting to build a Jewish house of worship in a Christian style of architecture; a quaint, mosquelike style became the preferred treatment for American temples. The Isaac M. Wise Synagogue in Cincinnati, built during the Civil War, even features mock minarets.

Florida boasts the largest American-Oriental building; the Tampa Bay Hotel with its many minarets and a grand porch of gingerbread horseshoe arches dates from the eighteen eighties. It now houses the University of Tampa.

UNIVERSITY OF TAMPA

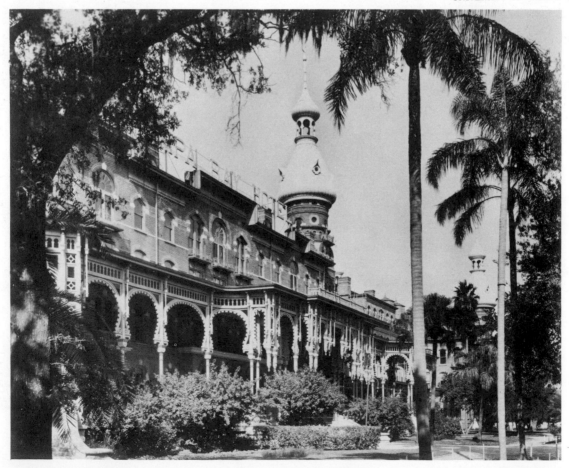

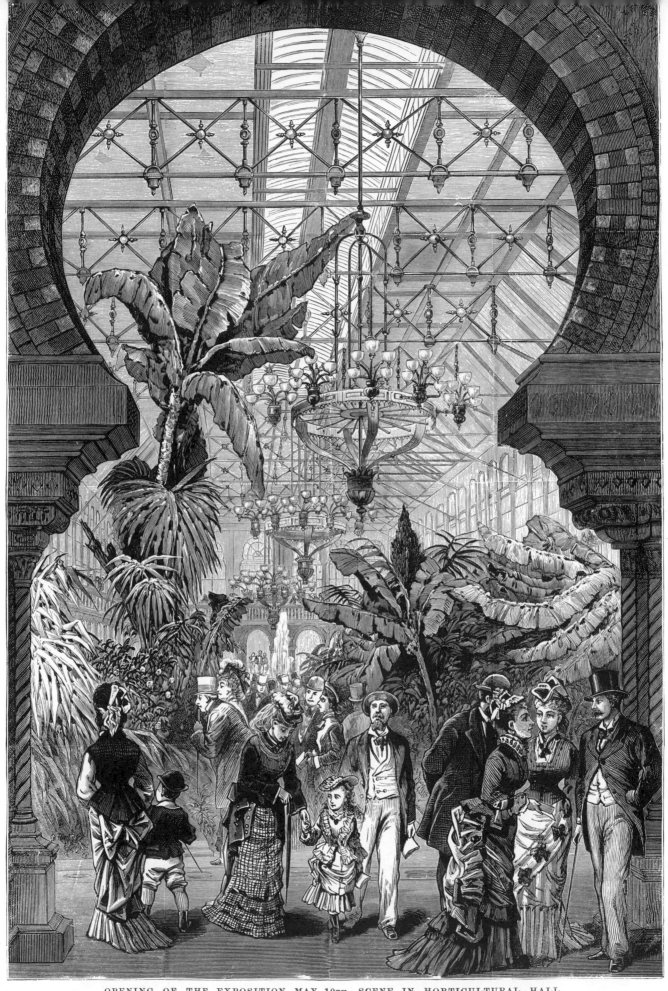

OPENING OF THE EXPOSITION, MAY 10TH—SCENE IN HORTICULTURAL HALL.

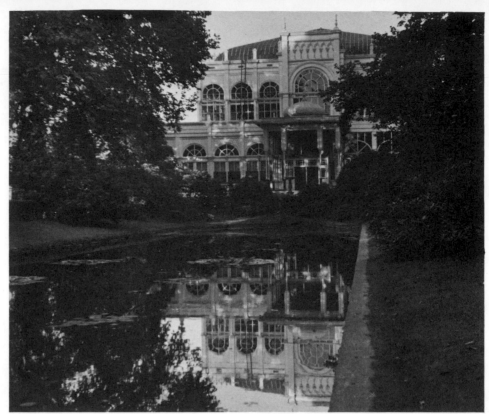

Horticultural Hall was a great "Saracenic Style" hothouse in Philadelphia's Fairmount Park, built for the Centennial Exposition of 1876. Herman J. Schwarzman, a little-known young landscape architect, designed this enchanted palace of iron, glass and colored brick. Black-and-white pictures fail to convey its marvelous effects of space and color; a grand vault of glass let in the sunlight to play on tropical flowers; Horticultural Hall gleaming in the moonlight by the reflecting pool was a vision to rival the Taj Mahal. After suffering very slight damage in a hurricane, this masterpiece of American Victorian design was wantonly torn down in 1955.

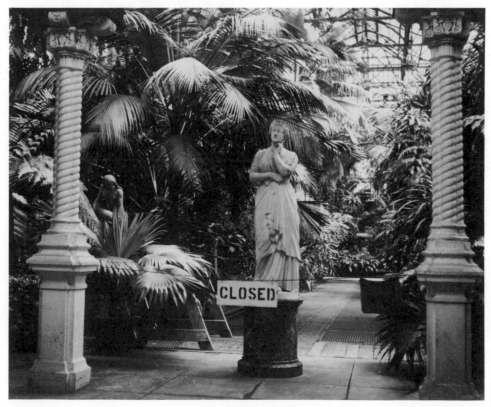

Oriental Villa

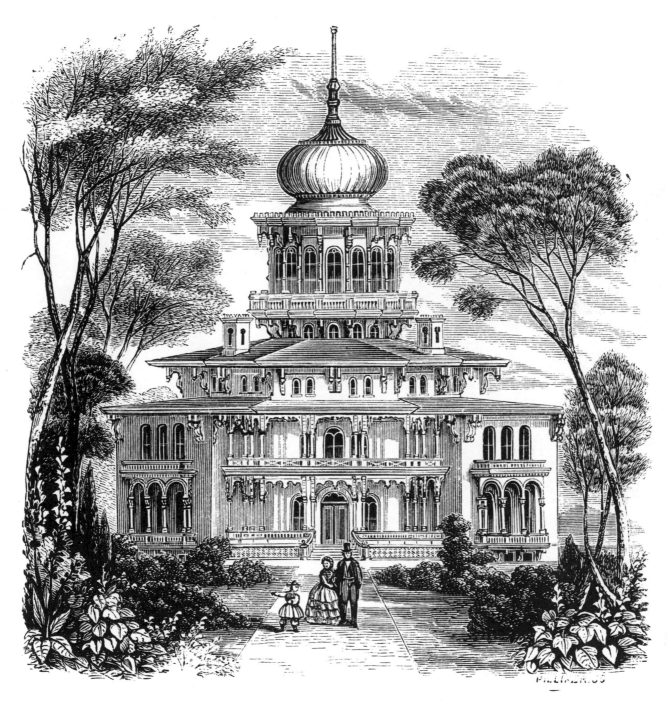

The most luxuriant flower of American-Oriental Architecture was to have been Longwood, designed by the Philadelphia architect Samuel Sloan for the planter Haller Nutt at Natchez, Mississippi. Sloan probably thought of this commission when he wrote, "Southerners have been known to travel fifteen hundred miles to see a handsome new house. The next thing was to outdo it, at whatever expense and in this they generally succeeded."

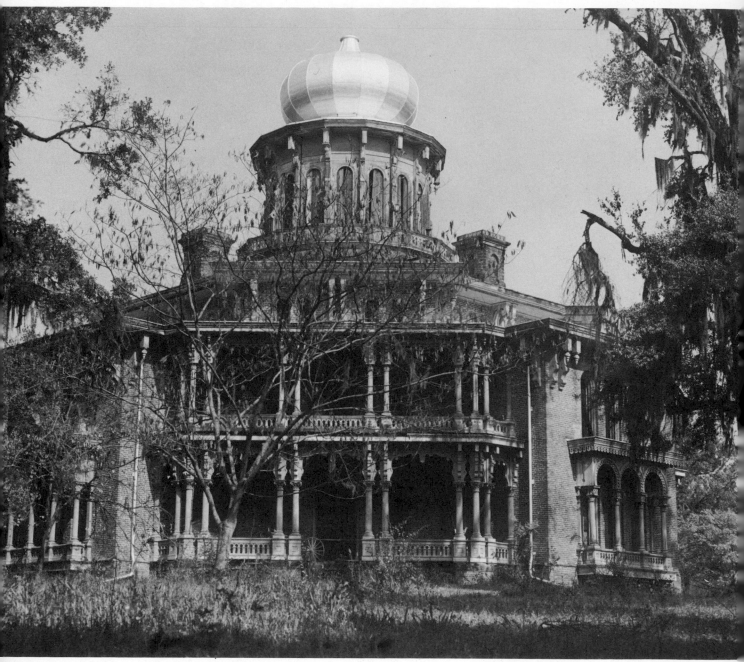

The Northern workmen left at the outbreak of the Civil War and Longwood's master died soon afterwards. The shell of this great pleasure dome still stands in a somber grove of trees hung with Spanish moss. It is now known as Nutt's Folly.

54

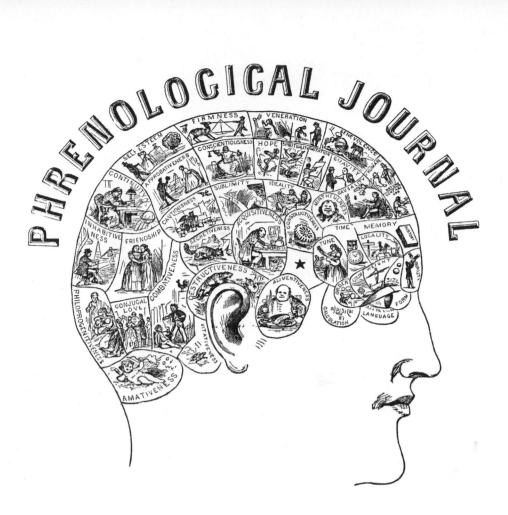

PHRENOLOGICAL JOURNAL

Eight-sided Longwood belongs to the orbit of Orson Squire Fowler and his Octagons. Fowler was a man in the grand and continuing American tradition of spellbinding crackpots. His specialty was phrenology, the pseudo science of reading character from skull bumps. Fowler also wrote *Sexual Science,* a frank marriage manual of 930 pages. Putting into practice his theories on "promoting sexual vigor" and "increasing female passion," Fowler married three times and he fathered three children when he was over seventy years old. Fowler did not actually invent the Octagon; there had been polygonal buildings for centuries, including some eight-sided churches, meeting houses, schools, tollhouses and barns in the United States. He pointed out the undeniable fact that eight walls enclose more space than four walls of the same length and insisted that an octagonal house was the one answer to each and every building problem. Fowler's book *A Home For All, or the Gravel Wall and Octagon Mode of Building, New, Cheap, Convenient, Superior and Adapted to Rich and Poor* was published in 1854. Hundreds of Octagons were built from Maine to California; an exact count of octagonal buildings has been made in New York State — 126 are still standing.

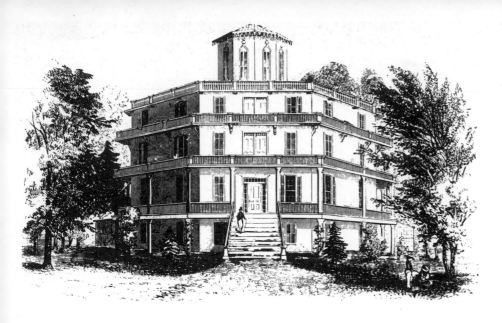

The eccentric Fowler had some sound ideas on housing; he was one of the first men to plan for central heating, gas lighting, hot and cold running water and indoor flush toilets. His own home was this huge Octagon at Fishkill, N.Y.; it was demolished in 1897.

The interior layout of eight-sided houses presented something of a problem. Each builder figured out his own way of dealing with the left over wedge-shaped spaces; they also found that every fashionable architectural style could be applied to the exterior of an Octagon. Here is a domed fantasy of 1860 at Irvington-on-Hudson, New York.

CARL CARMER

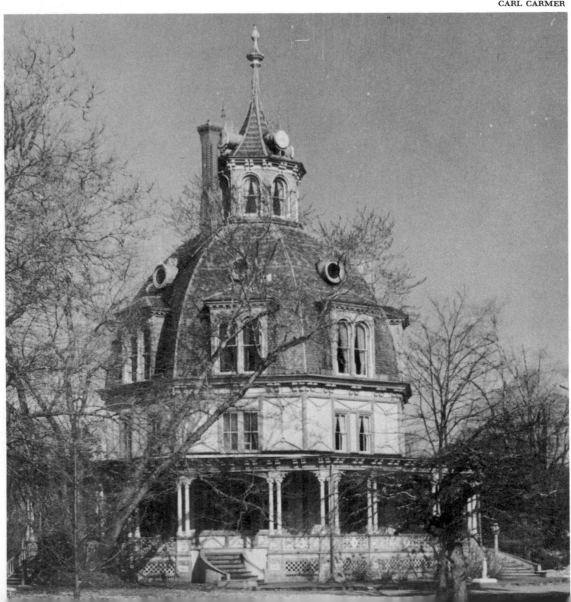

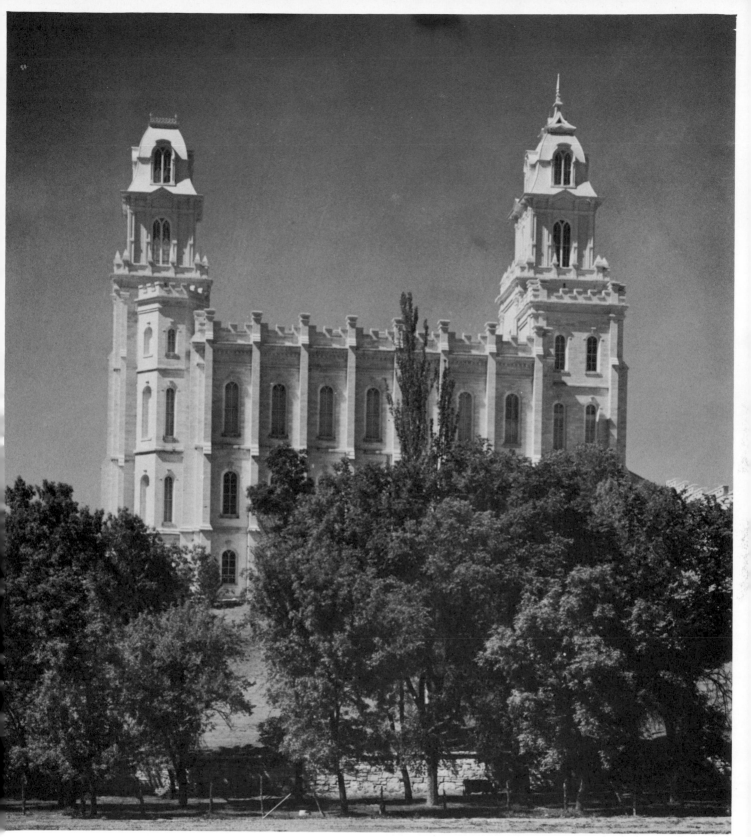

The Mormons developed an original style of architecture for their new religion. The Great Temple at Salt Lake City is famous; this stunning building is the little known Mormon Temple in the small town of Manti, Utah.

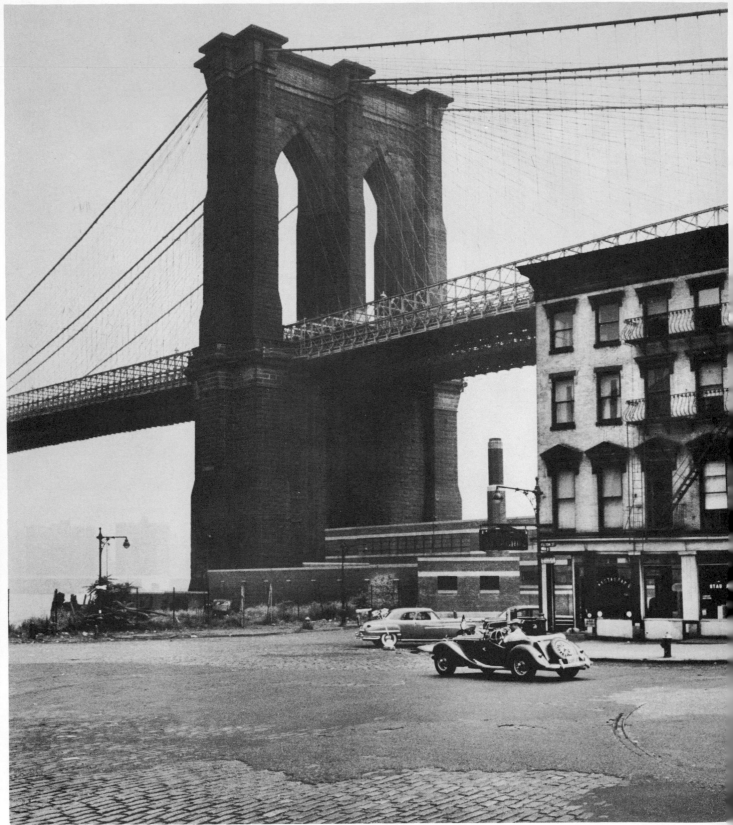

The pointed arches of these towers have been called "Gothic" but the Brooklyn Bridge created its own style. Combining romantic beauty and technical progress, it stands as the perfect symbol and crowning masterpiece of Victorianism. The contrast of massive stone against the tracery of tensed steel has fascinated more people than any other man-made structure in America.

CHAPTER 3

American Gothic

*Many persons of pure taste are
frightened when the idea of
"Gothic" is presented to them as
the style suggested for their home.*

— GERVASE WHEELER

No sight was more enchanting to the Victorians than a broken castle or a ruined abbey. Affluent European romantics even built artificial ruins in their gardens*. Unfortunately America had no medieval relics at all but brand-new Gothic buildings began to rise all over the United States in the eighteen thirties.

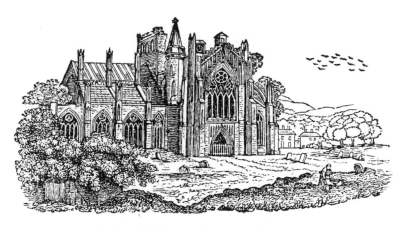

Ruins of Melrose Abbey, Roxburghshire.

Melrose Abbey, built about 700 years ago, was the finest Gothic structure in Scotland. It is 258 feet long, and 138 wide. These ruins are much admired, and are often visited by travellers.

This Gothic Revival in architecture was literary and sentimental in origin:

> We of this Saxon race feel somehow always a home-whispering voice at the heart when we gaze upon some crumbling beauty of Gothic Art in our nation's birth place across the ocean, different and more dear than the emotions that fill our souls in Greece or Italy.

Most Americans had of course never gazed upon England, Greece or Italy but they did like the new "Gothic cottages."

* A few rich Americans also had artificial ruins on their estates: John Church Cruger on Cruger's Island in the Hudson River, William Gilmor at Glen Ellen near Baltimore and Jay Cooke at Ogontz near Philadelphia. The latter two have disappeared.

61

The Victorians claimed that Gothic architecture was "organic" and based on the same principle as natural plant growth. The Gothic Revival in architecture is closely tied to the informal or "English" garden. It is no coincidence that Andrew Jackson Downing, the Gothic manner's chief herald in America, was a horticulturist by profession. Downing's real life story reads exactly like a Romantic Victorian novel:

Andrew is the son of a humble gardener in a Hudson River town. His father dies early and the boy leaves school and goes to work at the same trade. By chance he meets a Foreign Nobleman (the Baron Von Liederer) who takes a liking to the earnest lad and introduces him to society. At a nearby estate (Locust Grove), the tall, dark and handsome young man woos and wins a lovely heiress (Miss Caroline De Windt). He builds his bride a Gothic villa (Highland Gardens) in a pretty town overlooking a beautiful river (Newburgh-on-the-Hudson). He becomes a celebrity in his chosen field; he travels to Europe and meets the aristocracy; the President of the United States (Millard Fillmore) asks him to landscape the White House grounds. At the age of thirty-seven and the height of his fame, he boards a river boat for a short journey. The reckless shipowner starts a race with a rival captain

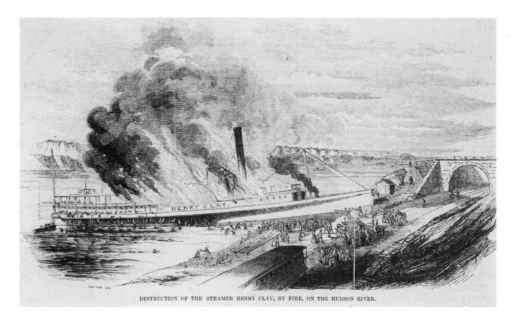

DESTRUCTION OF THE STEAMER HENRY CLAY, BY FIRE, ON THE HUDSON RIVER.

and the steamer catches fire. Downing succeeds in rescuing Caroline but, trying to save a beautiful young widow (Matilda Wadsworth), he dies a hero's death.

Downing lacked architectural training and he was fortunate in having Alexander Jackson Davis for a friend and collaborator*. Davis very aptly called himself an "architectural composer." He was also an accomplished artist; it is hard to imagine any client turning down a design presented by Davis in the form of a beguiling watercolor painting. Davis excelled in Gothic extravaganzas with turrets, battlements, pinnacles, crockets and oriels like Murray Hill, the New York mansion of W. H. Coventry Waddell. An admirer in the eighteen fifties commented:

> Vines are creeping around the tower, as they should around every Gothic tower, in order to make it effective. The trees cover the architectural beauty, making it more rare, more bewitching and enticing than if it appeared exposed.

When this house was demolished, Davis salvaged a spiral staircase and installed it in his own home, Wildmont.

The number of full-blown Gothic stone mansions was never large; some have disappeared, others now house private schools. Only wealthy men could afford such homes which required the labors of highly skilled stone carvers. But the costly Gothic style could be translated into wood, and thousands of "Carpenter Gothic" houses still stand. These characteristic Americana have steep gables and pointed windows; sometimes they were sheathed with vertical boarding instead of the familiar horizontal clapboard. This "board and batten" design was considered particularly fitting for a Gothic cottage because of its "upward tendency."

In a wider sense we now apply the term "American Gothic" to all homes of typically Victorian design. These houses were revolutionary,

---

* Andrew Jackson Downing and Alexander Jackson Davis must not be confused with a Hudson Valley neighbor of theirs, Andrew Jackson Davis, the celebrated spiritualist.

63

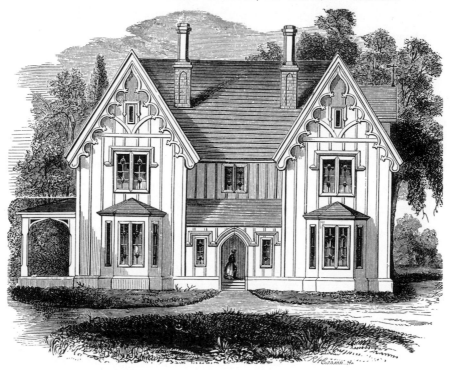

they mark the real beginning of modern architecture. The Greek Revival house was designed to fit behind a traditional facade, it belongs in a formal garden, is best viewed from the fixed standpoint of Renaissance perspective. The Victorian house broke free from this academic scheme. It is planned from the inside out, the free layout of rooms determines the outward look; the broken, "picturesque" exterior makes the most of the effects of sunlight, shade and foliage. These are good houses to walk around, to view at different times of day and year. Inside, they have a happy, hide-and-seek quality of surprise.

When Gothic was translated into "Carpenter Gothic," the stone tracery became wooden "gingerbread." This word is not of recent coinage or American origin: It goes back to the medieval French *gingimbrat* which meant preserved ginger. The last syllable was mistranslated into English as "bread." English gingerbread was a sort of cake, flavored with ginger and cut into fancy shapes. The word was then applied to the carved and gilded decoration of a sailing ship and

64

When we think of "Gothic," we think of churches. New York's Trinity Episcopal Church was completed in 1846 and made Richard Upjohn the most famous architect in America. Today the brownstone building is deep within the canyon of Wall Street.

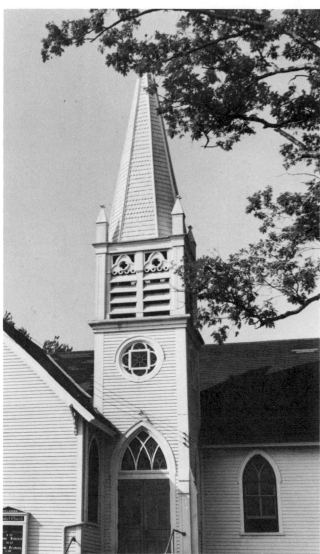

JOHN MAASS

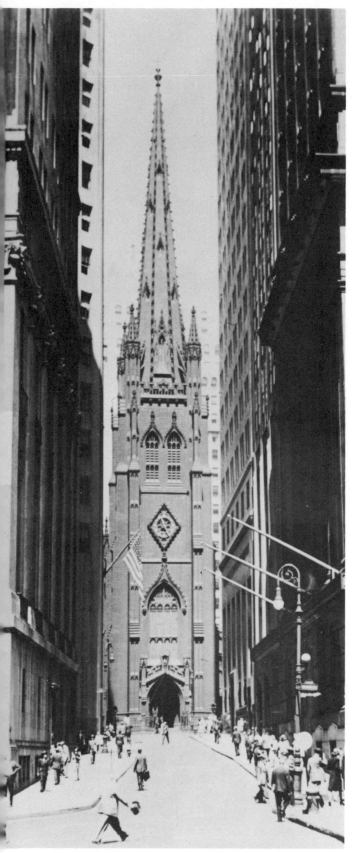

PARISH OF TRINITY CHURCH

Most Victorian Gothic city churches are rather grim — they suggest strict Sundays. But the homey Carpenter Gothic churches in the country are a delight. The design is often highly original and seems to have a touch of whimsy about it. Methodist Church, Mays Landing, New Jersey.

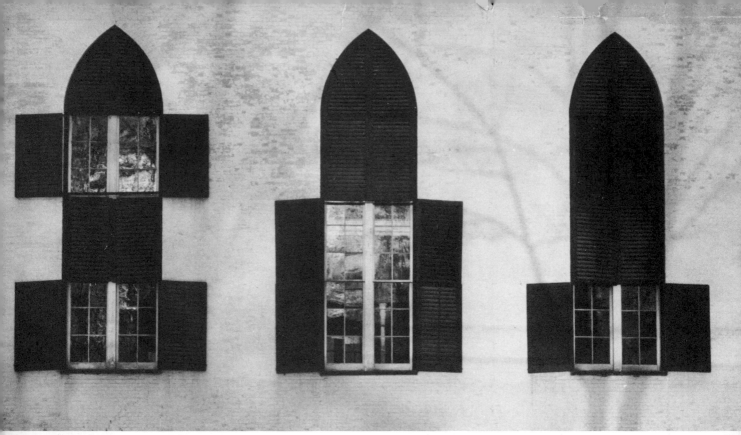

JOHN MAASS

A few examples of the wonderful variety of nineteenth century country churches:

A very early use of pointed Gothic windows in the Lutheran Church, Rhinebeck, New York.

A little red-and-white country church near Wellsboro, Pennsylvania.

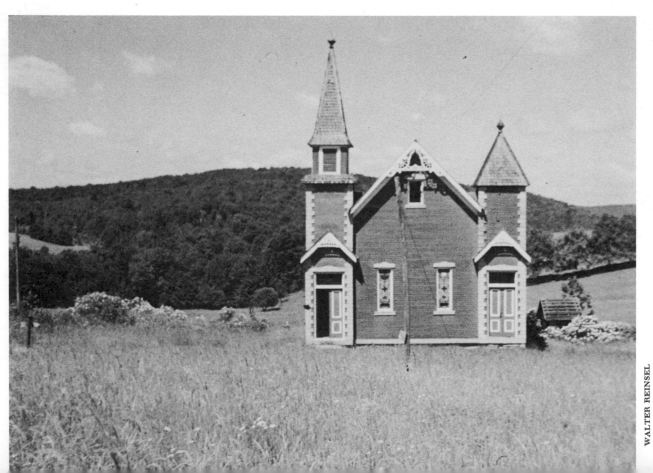

WALTER REINSEL

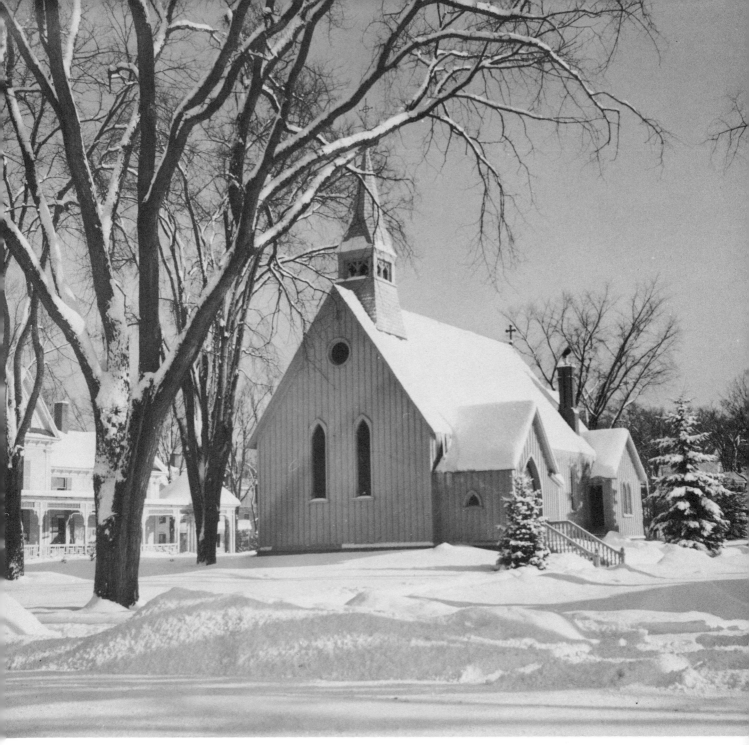

The Carpenter Gothic Episcopal Church at Hanover, New Hampshire.

69

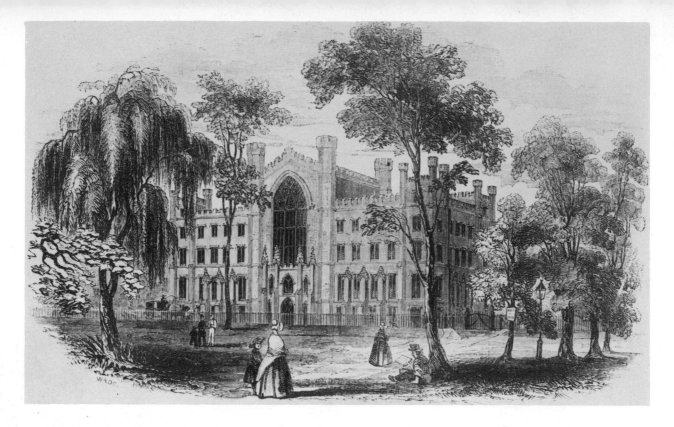

The earliest examples of "Collegiate Gothic" are the most attractive. New York University's building with its great chapel window on Washington Square was completed in the thirties and demolished in the nineties; the white marble for it was quarried by the convicts of Sing Sing. The University's professor of painting and sculpture roomed here; in 1837 he invited his friends to the demonstration of an interesting apparatus he had made. His name was Samuel Finley Breese Morse.

How to combine Collegiate Gothic and a mansard roof in one building; constructed in the seventies of green serpentine stone, it is now fortunately covered with ivy.

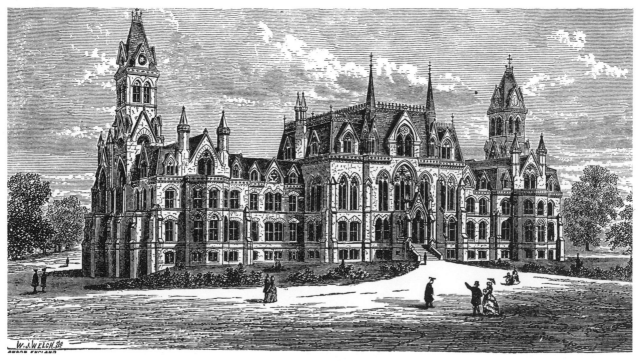

UNIVERSITY OF PENNSYLVANIA—DEPARTMENT OF ARTS AND SCIENCES.

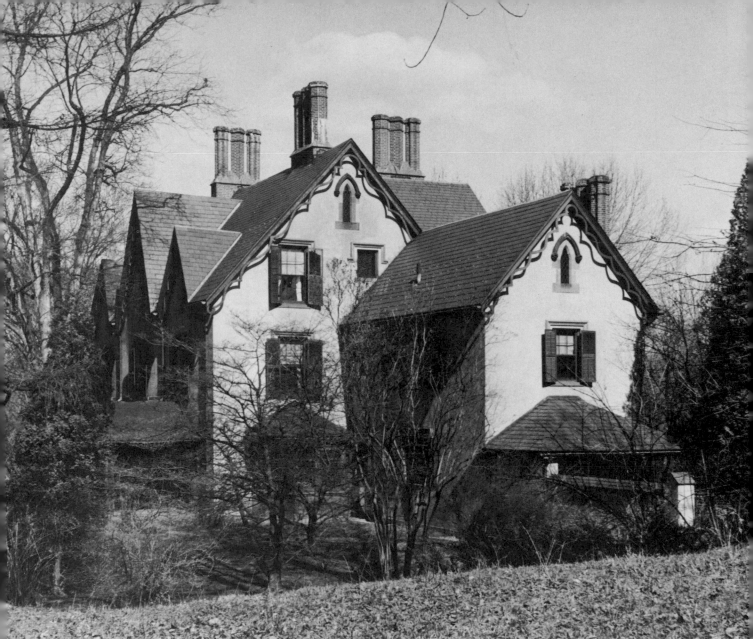

A Gothic stone mansion at Hartford, Connecticut. The wooden edging under the gables is patterned after the Tudor houses of England; it is called a vergeboard or bargeboard.

71

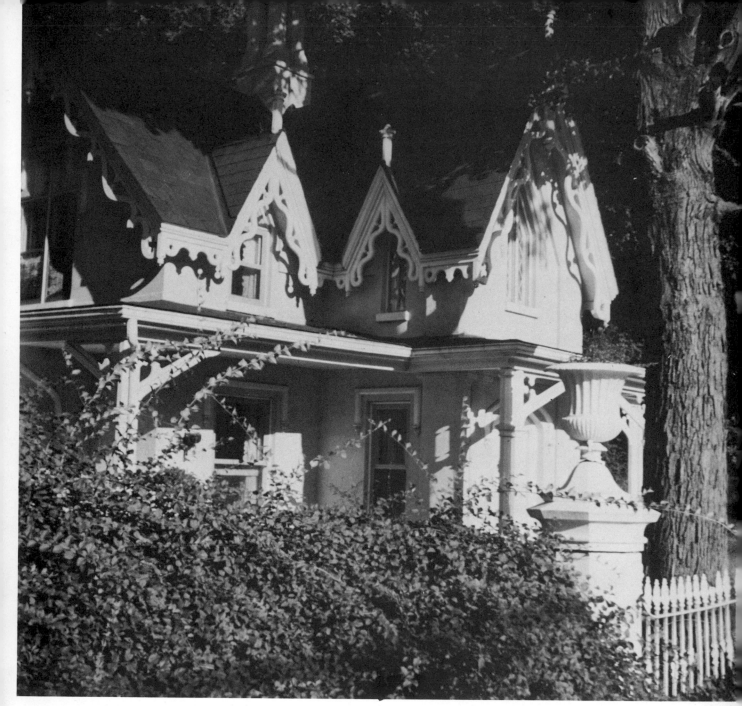

Matthew Vassar, a brewer of Poughkeepsie, New York, built his home, Springside, in the fifties. An admirer wrote in 1857: "We turn into an open gateway, pass a very neat and tasty gate-lodge, and here we are in a perfect paradise of beauties . . . a lasting monument to the genius of Downing and the liberality and taste of its proprietor Mr. Vassar who with a generosity equal to his taste permits the public to enjoy the charms he has created." This pink-and-white delight is the gate lodge.

Downing wrote: "Veranda, Piazza or Colonnade is a necessary and delightful appendage to a dwelling house and in fact during a considerable part of the year, frequently becomes the lounging apartment of the family." This was Idlewild, the home of the writer Nathaniel P. Willis at Newburgh-on-the-Hudson; it was designed by Downing's partner and successor Calvert Vaux.

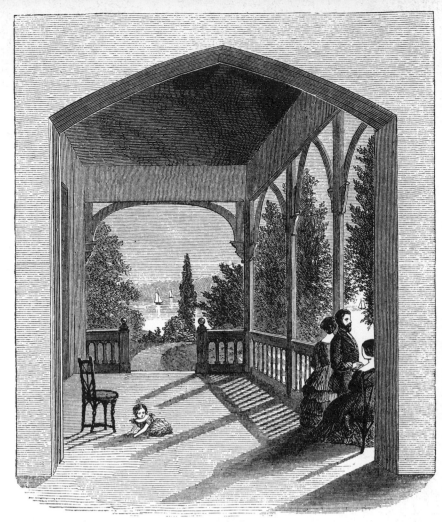

THE RIVER, EAST FROM THE PIAZZA.

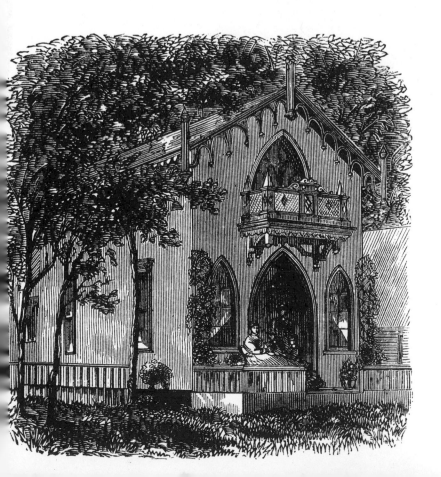

A Methodist camp meeting cottage on Martha's Vineyard, Massachusetts. In 1868 a reporter wrote: "There are over 200 cottages on the ground. In front there is a pretty little veranda, and three or four feet of garden may be fenced in before it. Over the front door there is generally a balcony. The high-peaked roofs, the balconies, the door and window frames, are all decorated with scroll-work; stained glass, silver doorplates, hanging lanterns, and other luxuries are beheld at every turn; the houses are gayly painted, the verandas bloom with rare flowers, the little miniature yards are decked with moss and shell-work, and under the trees, which cast a thick shade over all, are rustic benches and swings for the children."

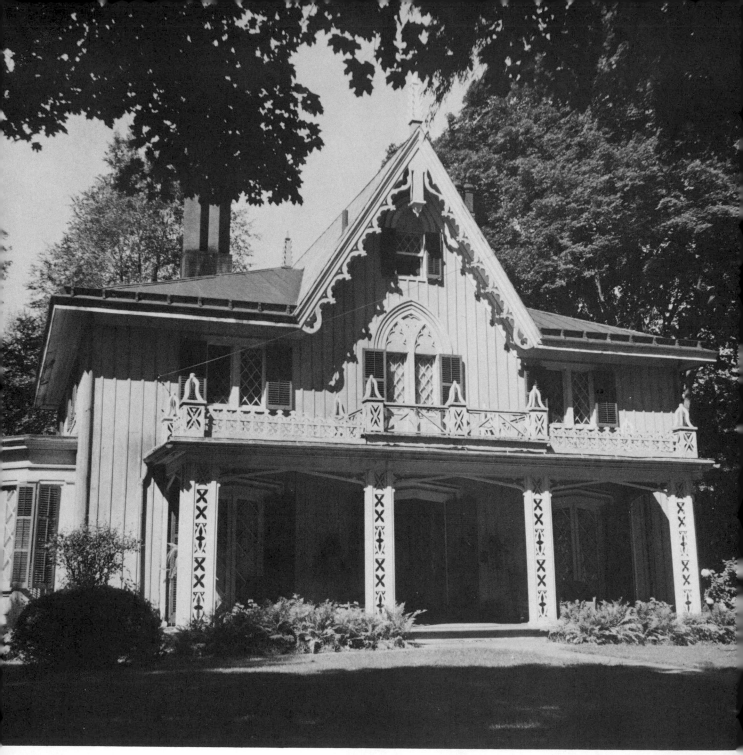

Alexander Jackson Davis, architect of great mansions, designed this graceful cottage at Rhinebeck, New York, a prototype for many such houses with a central gable.

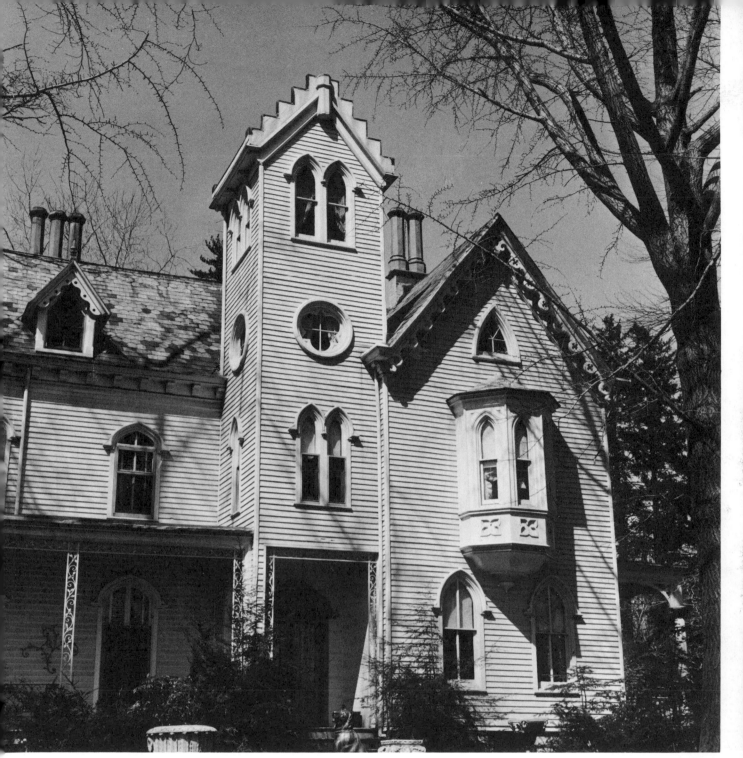

A handsome Carpenter Gothic mansion at Darien, Connecticut. It was built in the sixties for Fred W. Bruggerhoff, a merchant and state senator who often commuted to his New York office by sailboat.

75

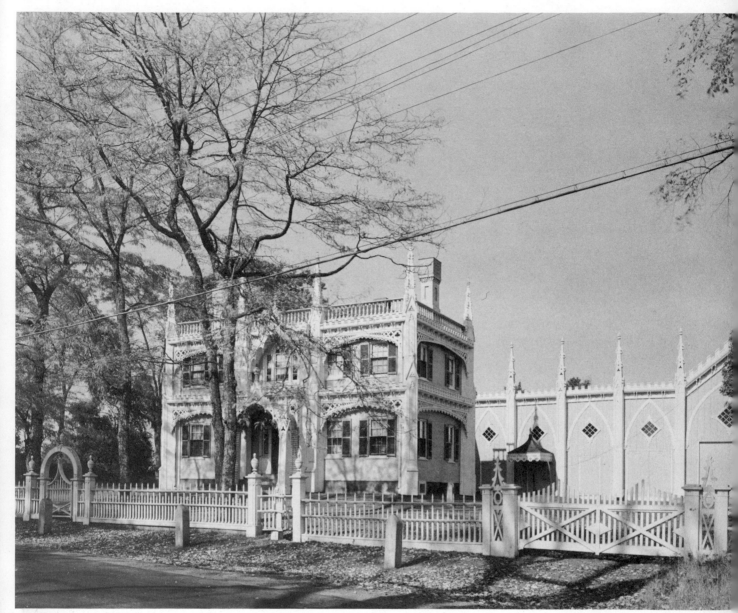

The so-called Wedding Cake House at Kennebunk, Maine. It belonged to a sea captain who made his foursquare home fashionable by adding the Gothic lacework.

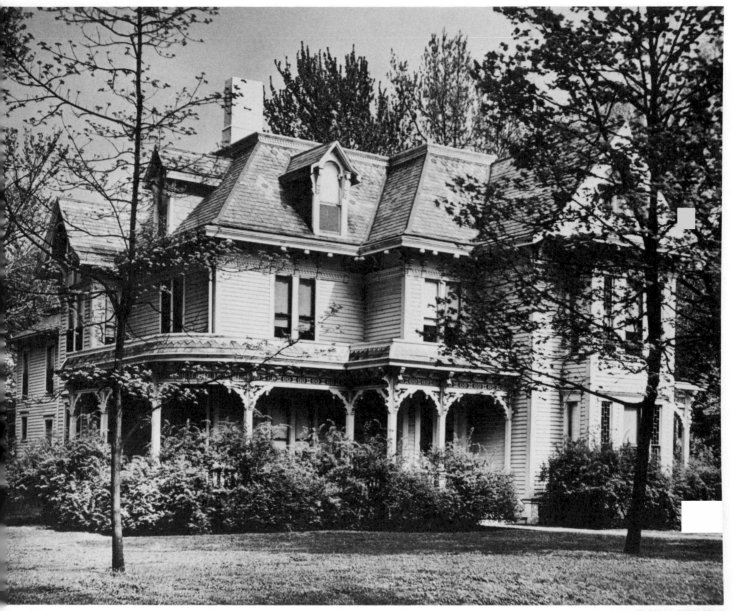

This fine example of a commodious Victorian residence has been in the same family since it was built in 1865. There are steep gables and a mansard roof, gingerbread under the eaves and on the porches, the bay window still has the now rarely seen panes of colored glass. It is the home of Mr. and Mrs. Harry S. Truman at Independence, Missouri.

77

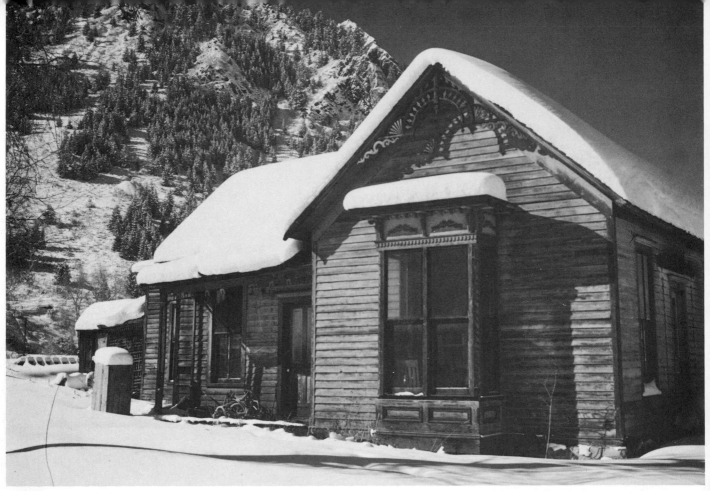

Two trim homes in the onetime silver-mining town of Aspen, Colorado.

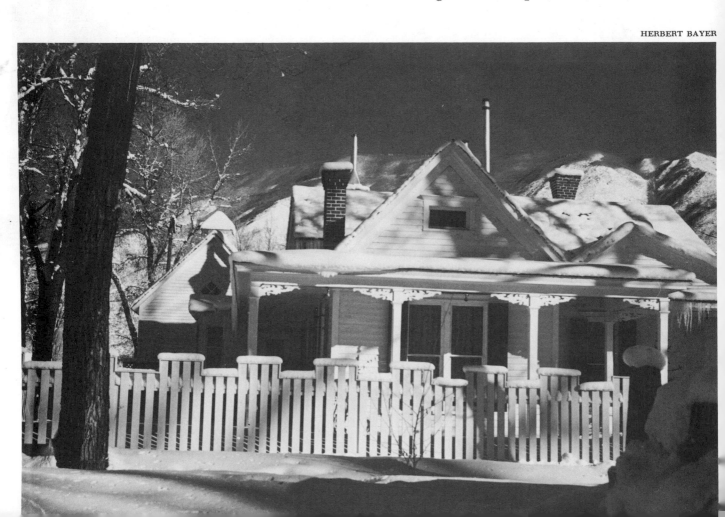

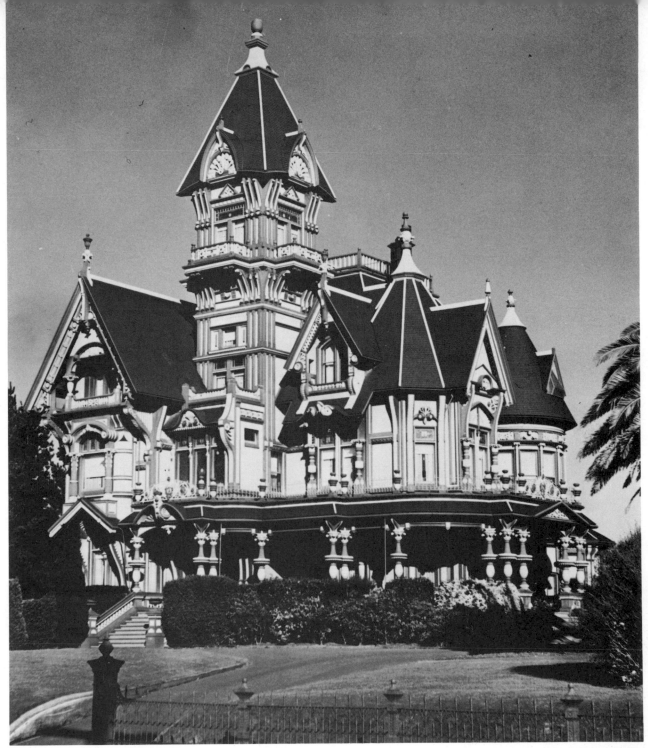

The "Carson Mansion" built in the eighties at Eureka in Northern California
has become famous because it is almost a parody on a Victorian house.
William Carson was a redwood pioneer who may have wanted to show off
the wonderful things that could be done with lumber.

79

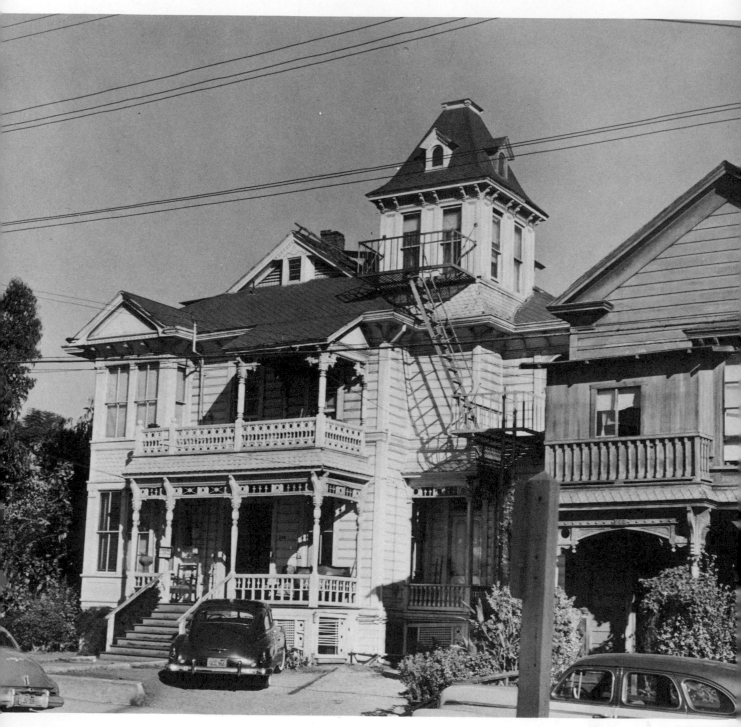

A dazzling house on Bunker Hill, Los Angeles.

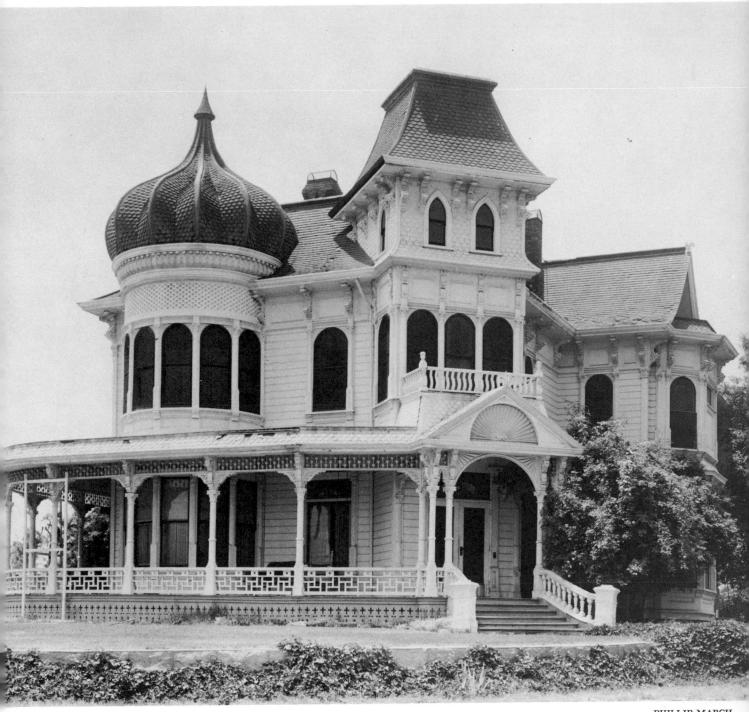

An extravaganza at Redlands in Southern California. Every detail — the strange tower and cupola, the shingles, the spindlework and Chinese railing on the porch — shows great inventiveness.

81

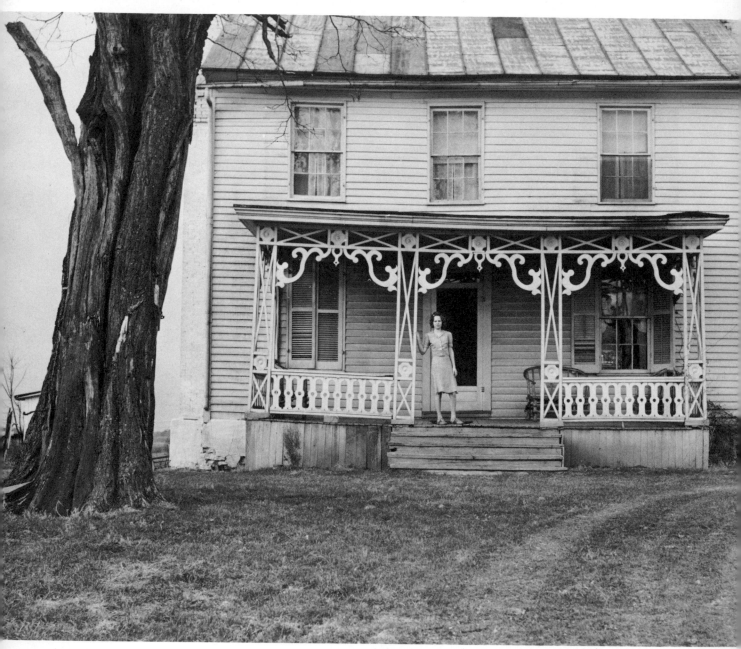

A porch in Nicholas County, Kentucky.

82

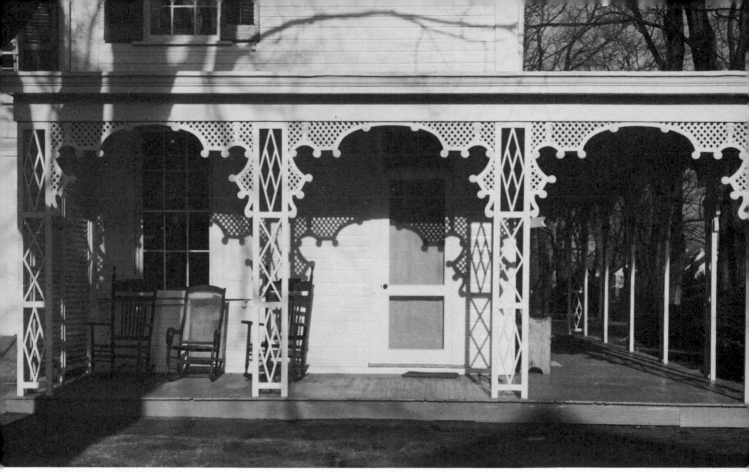

A cemetery superintendent lives here; Doylestown, Pennsylvania.

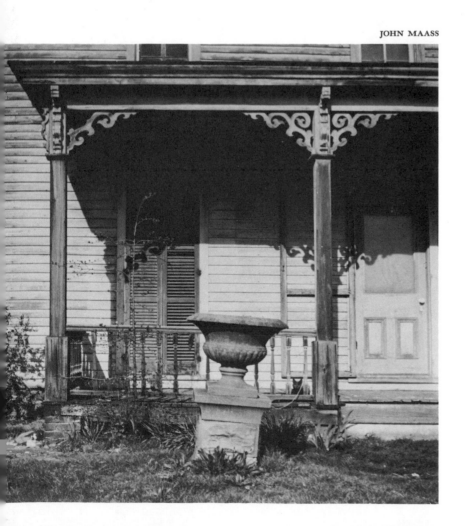

Even some farmhouses had an elegant cast-iron or terra-cotta vase out front; Gloucester County, N.J.

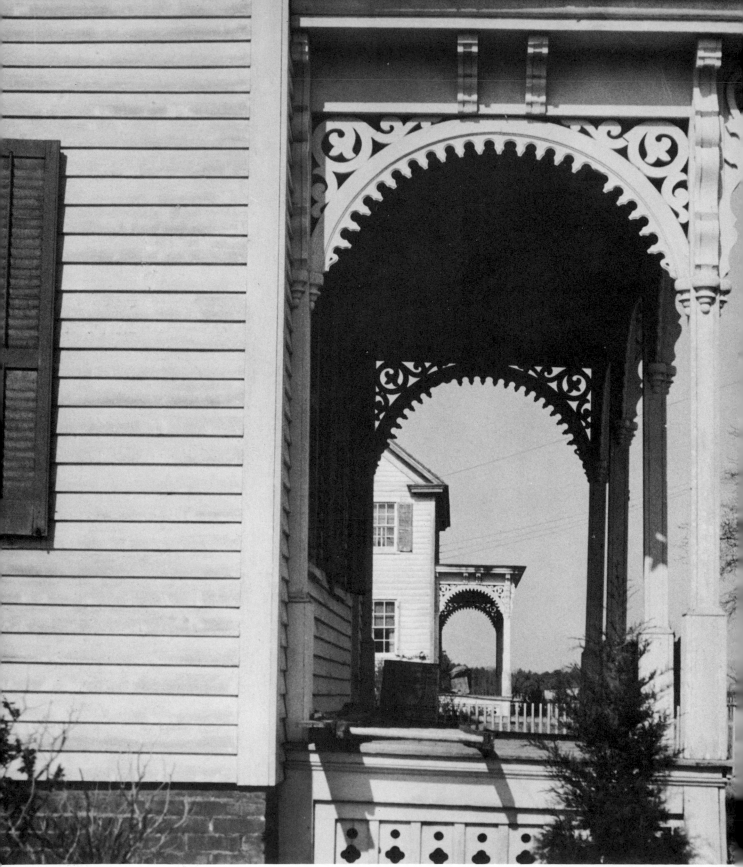

Three variations on a gingerbread theme in Cape May County, New Jersey.

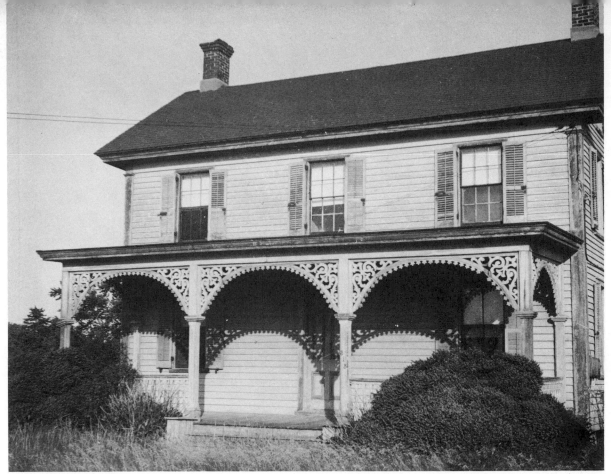

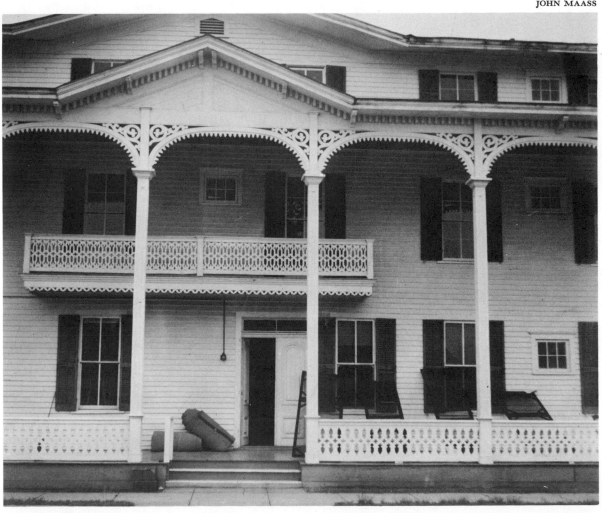

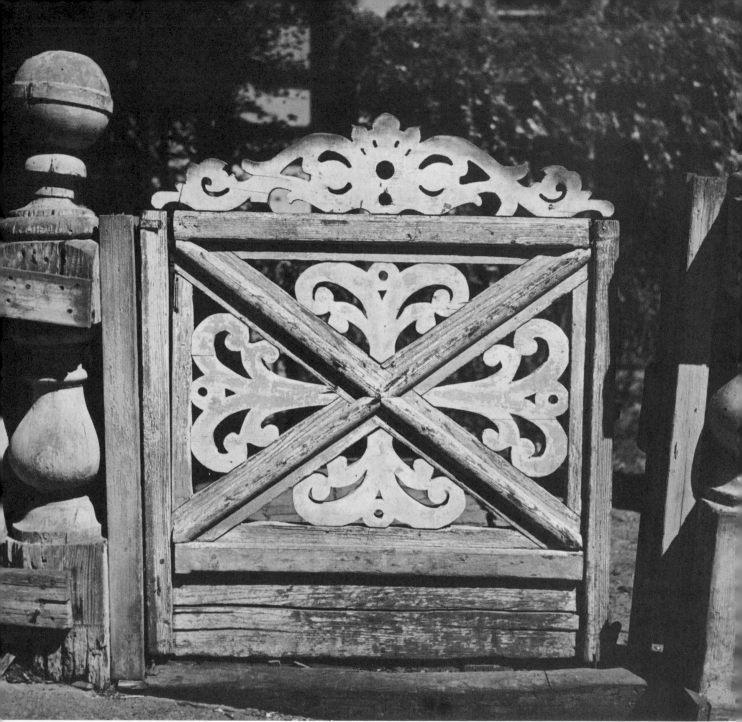

The gate to Humphrey's Castle on Russian Hill in San Francisco. During the Great Fire, the owner saved the house by wetting it down with champagne and seltzer water. The same story is told of Policeman Bellinger and the Chicago Fire but he used only apple cider to protect his humbler home.

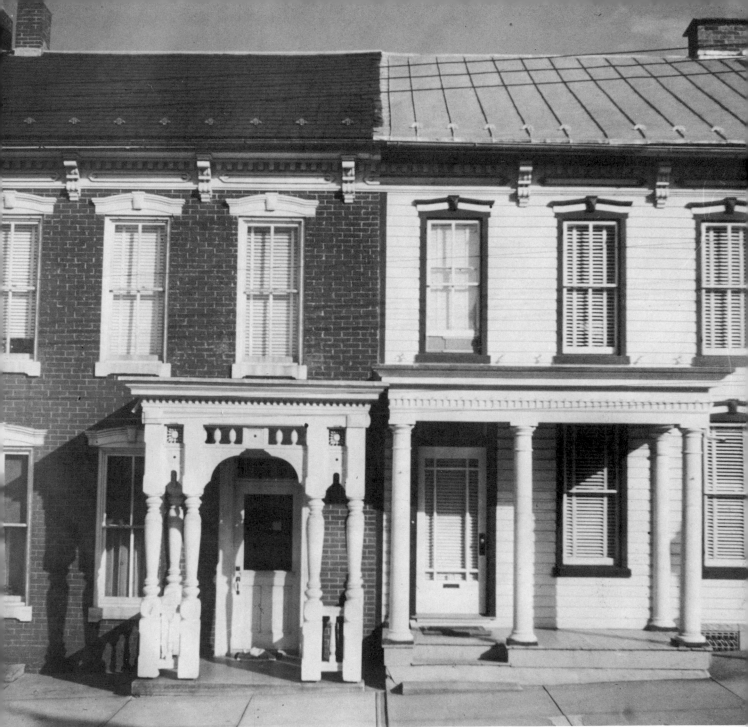

A little paint and gingerbread go a long way; the Victorians avoided monotonous streets by imaginative use of trim and color; two neighbors in Kutztown, Pennsylvania.

87

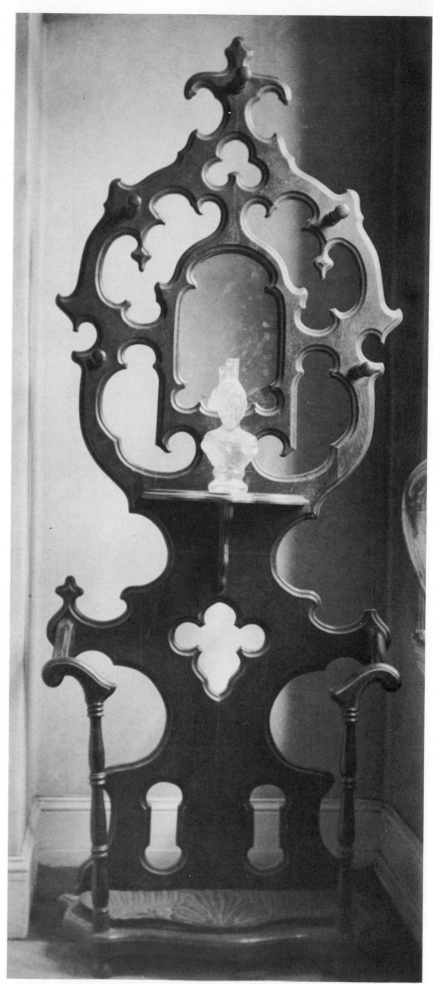

American Gothic furniture sometimes looks like architecture on a
small scale: a fanciful hatrack-
umbrella stand.

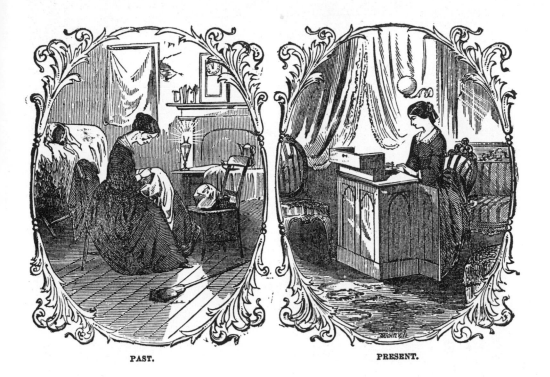

PAST.   PRESENT.

Gothic showed up in unexpected places like this sewing machine case.

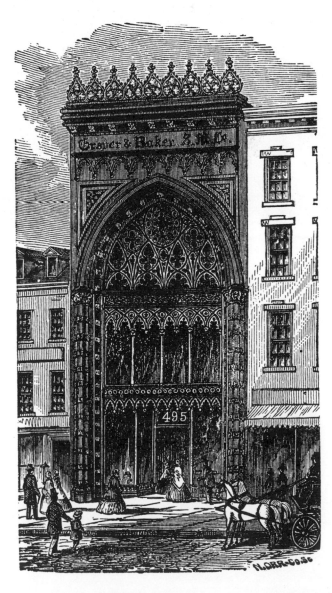

The showroom of the Grover & Baker Sewing Machine Company on New York's Broadway was an odd example of "Commercial Gothic."

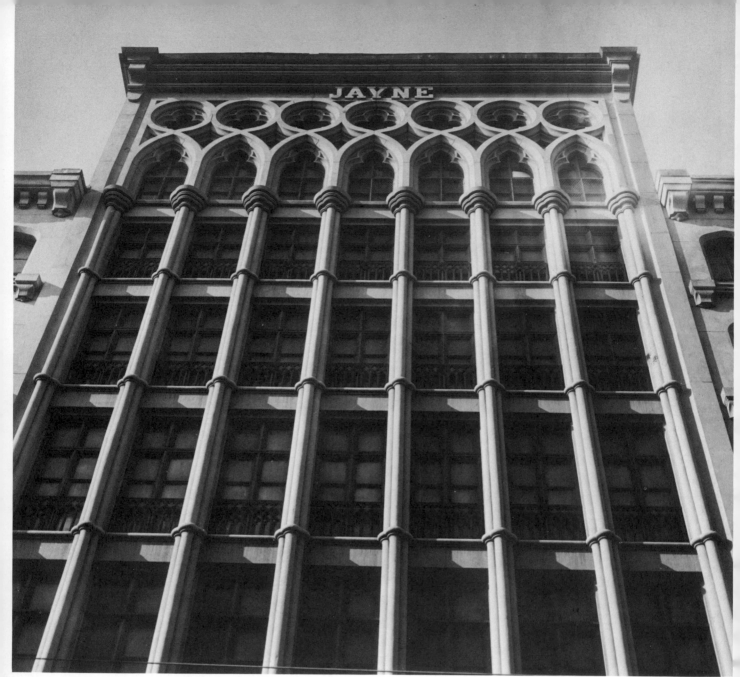

The Jayne Building in Philadelphia is America's oldest skyscraper. It was built in 1849 for the patent medicine manufacturer, Dr. David Jayne; the young architect, William Johnston, died during its construction. The Jayne Building has only eight stories above ground and two below street level but the soaring granite façade of "Venetian Gothic" design is still a most impressive sight. Johnston's successor added an observation tower and huge sculptured druggist's mortars above the eighth floor but these were destroyed by fire in 1872.

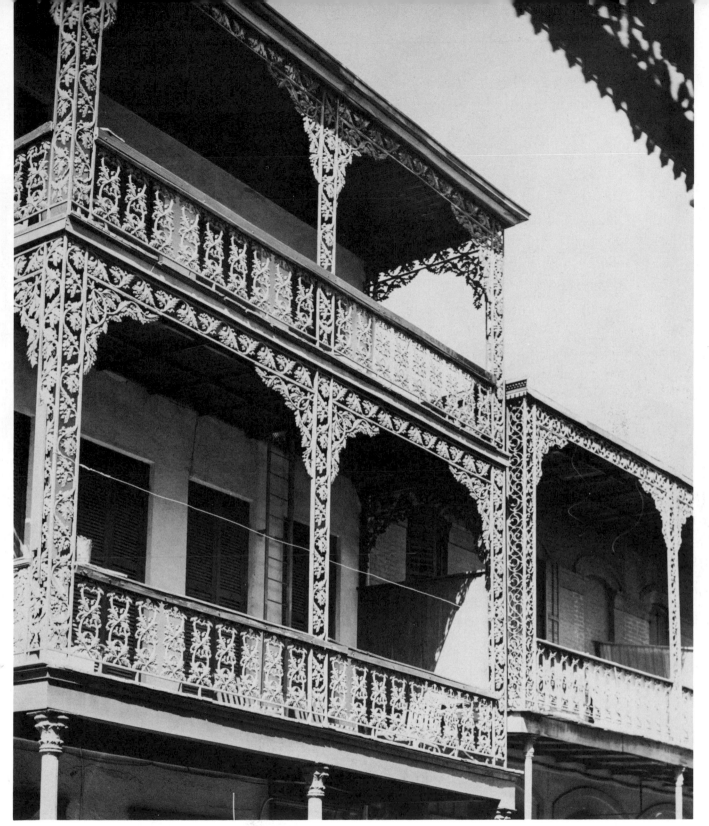

Ornamental ironwork is a counterpart to gingerbread; there are two kinds, the older wrought iron and the Victorian cast iron. Tourists are told that the celebrated ironwork of New Orleans is a flower of "French heritage" and "Creole craftsmanship." Actually, most of it was manufactured in Northern foundries which shipped their product all over the country. The same charming patterns may still be found in New York, Philadelphia, Baltimore and many smaller communities if you look for them.

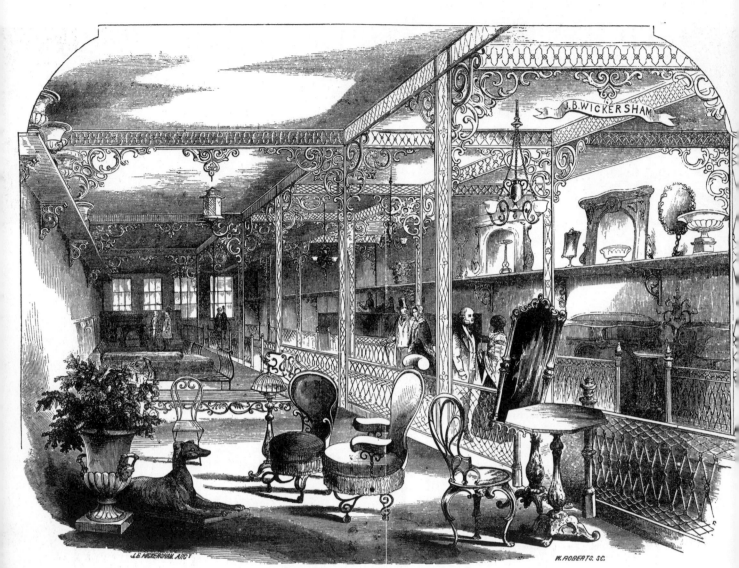

IRON WAREHOUSE OF JOHN B. WICKERSHAM, NO. 312 BROADWAY, NEW YORK.

Mr. Wickersham had introduced a process of manufacturing "woven iron" which was claimed to be stronger and lighter than cast iron. Here is a description of his showroom from the eighteen fifties: "There are farm-fences, wrought iron railings of superior strength and finish, gratings, ve-randahs, balconies, furniture of all kinds, bedsteads, statuary, settees, chairs, mantels, washstands, toilet-glasses, centre-tables, tree-guards, fountains, hat-stands, brackets and all other kinds of iron work. A ramble through a factory of this kind suggests thoughts of the amazing progress of American enterprise, industry and ingenuity, both grateful and stimulating to our national feelings."

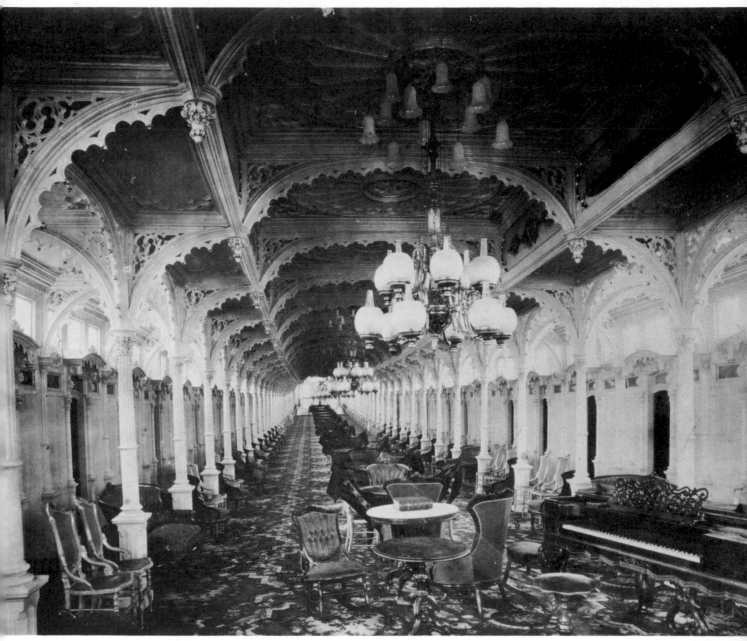

Gingerbread afloat: The grand salon of the Mississippi steamer *Great Republic*. The fancy Victorian style of Southern mansions is sometimes called "Steamboat Gothic."

93

Gingerbread abroad: Wooden fretwork and decoration on the outside of houses is a native folk art of many timber countries.

Right: The rugged houses of Alpine villages — known to Americans as "chalets" — are bright with ornamental woodwork. This is a farmhouse in Austria; the bell in the little rooftop spire calls in the hands at mealtime.

Below left: The houses of rural Russia are still built of logs today and eaves, porch and windows are trimmed with fretwork; the resemblance to Nineteenth Century American gingerbread buildings is quite startling.

Below right: The most exuberant and fantastic gingerbread architecture is found in the West Indies. A late nineteenth century villa at Port-au-Prince, Haiti.

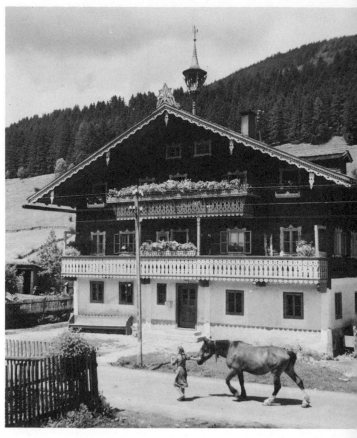

CAS OORTHUYS — CONTACT PUBLISHING COMPANY, AMSTERDAM

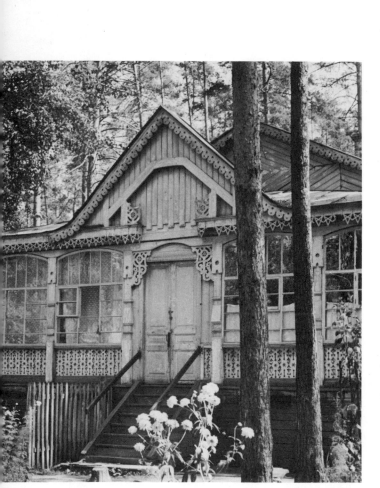

HENRI CARTIER-BRESSON

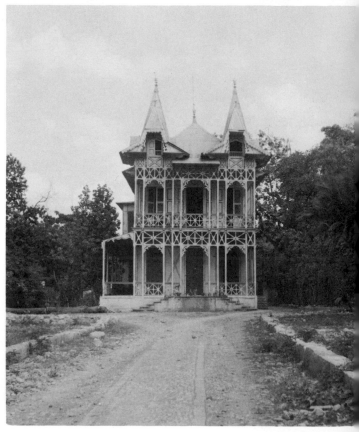

SELDEN RODMAN

CHAPTER 4

ITALIANATE INTERLUDE

*I have eaten good pears but I
long for grapes and figs.*
— GOETHE, *Italian Journey*

Italy has been loved by all nations in every time but none loved her more than the Anglo-Saxons of the romantic era. The early Victorians were convinced that "architecture is an art in which Italy has no modern rival. Though some of the northern nations may have erected more huge and more costly structures, none of them display the same high, pure and classical taste."

No wonder, gentlemen of means who aspired to culture were eager to enjoy some of this Italian refinement in their own homes. "Italian" or "Tuscan" villas had become popular in England* during the eighteen twenties and the fashion spread to America about ten years later. American Italianate houses are second cousins to the real villas of Italy; they were at first copied from the designs in English pattern books and several of the most successful Italian villa architects in the United States — Richard Upjohn, John Notman, Gervase Wheeler, Calvert Vaux — were recent immigrants from Britain.

The Italianate villa was in vogue until the eve of the Civil War and this brief period has left us beautiful and distinctive buildings. None of the clichés about dark, gloomy, fussy Victorian mansions can possibly be applied to these high, wide and handsome homes.

There is a timeless air of good design and good taste about these amazingly "modern" Victorian houses. Their ground plans are open and informal, featuring bay windows and sliding doors; the outward aspect is an interesting free arrangement of blocks and wings; the roofs have wide overhangs; the first floor rooms open on to terraces and loggias for outdoor living. All these amenities anticipate the same features in present-day houses by over a century!

The most delightful parts of American Italian villas are their towers; they are frankly for pleasure, "affording a cool retreat where the breeze blows unmolested and whence a cheerful and extended prospect

* Queen Victoria built two country homes. The first was Osborne, a very large Italian villa, the second Balmoral, a castle in the "Scottish Baronial" manner. Her husband designed both of them.

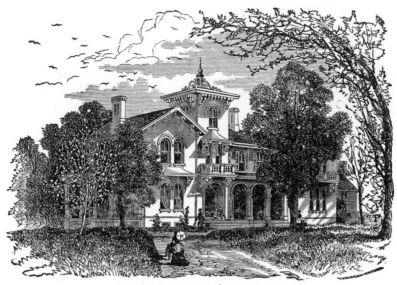

EX-GOVERNOR ROSS' RESIDENCE.

is commanded." The proprietor of a Hudson Valley Villa turned his tower into a billiard room.

A second distinctive type of Italianate villa is shaped like a cube with a lookout atop the flat roof. This jaunty feature is known in different parts of the country as "cupola," "observatory" or "belvedere." It is not to be confused with the New England "widow's walk" which was an open, railed platform over a peaked roof. These lookouts are architecture for the fun of it; one of the few "practical" uses for it was recorded by a clergyman who wrote his sermons in this secluded place. The belvedere is usually reached by a trapdoor and is topped by a scrolled "finial" which forms the base of a flagpole or weather vane — now usually replaced by a television antenna.

This style from tree-poor Italy is of course typical masonry architecture; the first American Italian villas were the urban or suburban homes of wealthy men, very dignified in design and built of stone. Few people could afford the expense of a stone villa so the somewhat austere Italian style was Americanized by translating the designs into the familiar and less costly frame and clapboard construction. Even arches, roundheaded windows and carved moldings were cheerfully executed

98

in wood. Gingerbread, scrollwork, shutters and trim were applied to the body of the house and painted in bright colors. The brackets under the cornice grew larger and fancier until this delightful Americanized Italian style became known as "Hudson River Bracketed."*

The same period also saw the rise of the "town house" with its vaguely Italian detail. Blocks of these tall houses still stand in most larger cities, the notorious "brownstone" is the best known example of the style. The brownstone houses were built of brick, faced with slabs of chocolate-colored red sandstone or freestone. A balustraded "stoop" leads up to the raised first floor. Most New York brownstones have two parlors, kitchen in front on ground floor and dining room on the garden. The "brownstone" is a house with very respectful manners: The "company rooms" on the first floor have the highest ceilings and the tallest windows; as we mount from story to story, the rooms have less and less headroom. Father and Mother resided on the second floor; the children slept on the third floor, servants and spare rooms took up the top floor. A gentleman who was born in a Brooklyn brownstone writes:

> I remember a formidable extension dining room with a stained-glass skylight. The skylight leaked. . . . I remember the laundry where the pipes froze solid every winter, the bathtub apparently built for a race of midgets, the furnace which devoured 30 tons of coal every winter but heated only the cellar . . . the façade had gargoyles. The basement gate clanged like the Bastille. . . . The Brownstone was large but not roomy. It was fancy but not beautiful. It was orderly in a littered sort of way. It was consistent in that nothing belonged where it was.

In fairness we must realize that the brownstone was designed as a single-family residence and it was certainly ample for that purpose. Later, many of them were cut up into small apartments or single rooms

---

* Edith Wharton wrote a novel entitled *Hudson River Bracketed* with fine descriptions of a fictional mansion, The Willows.

for rent. Memories of living on a budget, sleeping on a sofa, cooking on a gas ring and telephoning in a hallway have made the brownstone a symbol of urban frustration.

The Italianate period left a lasting imprint on American official and commercial architecture. Grecian buildings were costly and it was almost impossible to enlarge them. An "astylar"* building in the Italian style was more efficient and could be added to in all directions if the need arose.

Beginning in the eighteen thirties, many banks, insurance company offices, the first department stores, city halls, schools, libraries and railroad stations were designed in a style patterned after Italian palazzos. This Renaissance manner remained popular in America for a hundred years, growing more and more ornate all the time. The strong, clean-cut pre-Civil War examples are far more attractive than the overblown imitations from the Beaux Arts period.

Many hundreds of commercial buildings with arched windows and strong moldings** still stand near the water fronts of American cities. The bold facades are festooned with a hovering web of fire escapes; on weekends when these streets are deserted, they look like giant stage sets.

Cast-iron buildings also assumed Renaissance façades; James Bogardus of New York was the inventor, though the occasional use of iron as a building material goes back to the very beginning of the Industrial Revolution. Many advantages were claimed for the cast-iron buildings:

> In resisting any kind of strain, it is vastly superior to stone or brick. Practically, cast-iron is crushing proof for a column must be ten miles in height before it will crush itself by its own weight.

---

* An architect's word used to impress clients — it means "without columns."

** The moldings and cornices cast shadows and give variety within unity of scale to a street of Victorian commercial buildings. Present-day buildings which hide their structure under a flat skin are often monotonous and inferior in this respect.

100

ITALIANATE INTERLUDE

We think of prefabrication as an ultramodern process but the manufacture of prefabricated buildings — both in wood and in iron — was a flourishing nineteenth century industry:*

> A front of iron can be prepared and fitted in the manufactory and thence transported to the place of erection and put together with wonderful rapidity and at all seasons of the year.

These cast-iron façades were certainly not "honest" design, they were deliberately made to look like stone fronts, but many of them are very handsome all the same.

Cast-iron buildings were claimed to be fire-proof.

> They are also perfectly safe during thunderstorms. The metal becomes a huge conductor and silently conveys all the electricity to the earth.

But the iron buildings turned out to be failures; they cost more than conventional buildings and had to be painted frequently to prevent rust. Cast iron loses its strength when it is exposed to heat and during the great fires of Chicago and Boston in the seventies, some iron buildings collapsed before they had been touched by flames. This killed the cast-iron building industry. The steel skeleton skyscraper came twenty years later.

* An iron harem for the 320 wives of King Eyambo on the Calavar River was made in England and shipped to Africa in 1843.

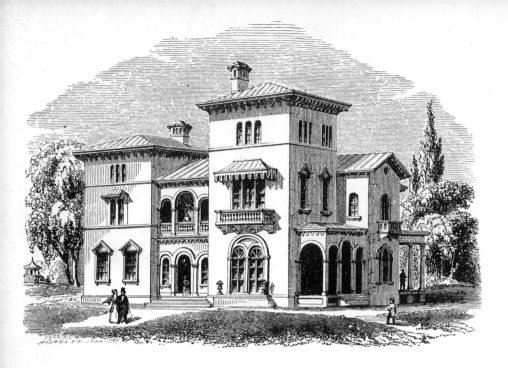

The Edward King House in elegant Newport, Rhode Island, is a mansion of 1845. Here are all the fashionable Italianate details — loggias, flattop tower and a balcony shaded by an oddly scalloped hood. This villa is now the People's Library.

Some years later William Wyman, a wealthy Baltimorean, built Homewood Villa, a copy of the King House on an even bigger scale. Johns Hopkins University was founded on land donated by Wyman. He also left his villa to the University which apparently did not appreciate the gift — it was torn down in 1955 to make room for a small parking lot.

JOHN MAASS

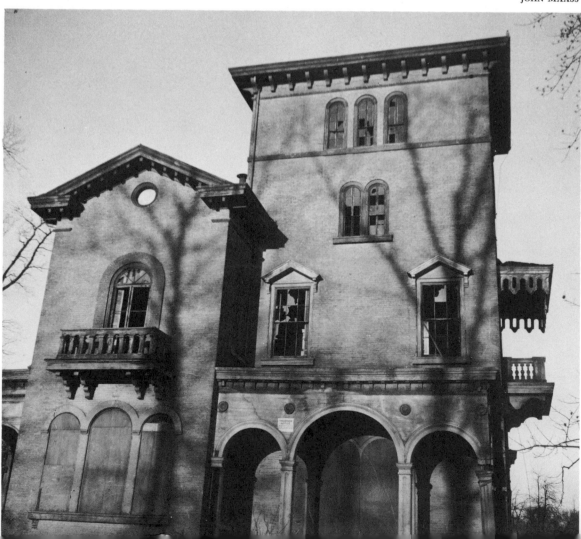

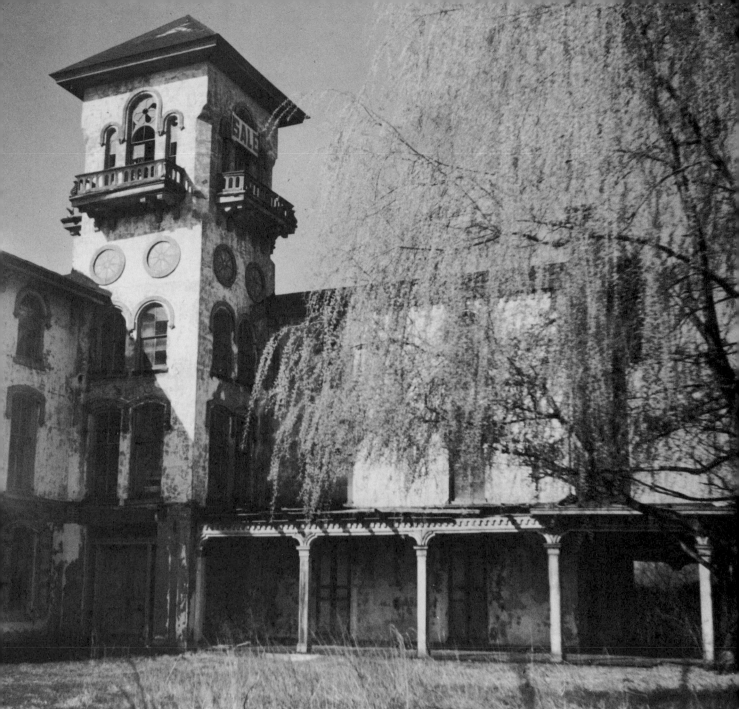

"Doctor" Joseph Hammett Schenck claimed to have learnt the secret of healing roots and herbs from an old Indian woman in New Jersey. He made his fortune in the sixties manufacturing Mandrake Pills and Seaweed Tonic, good for man or beast. His towering villa still stands among willow trees near Bristol, Pennsylvania. That SALE sign has been up there for a long time.

103

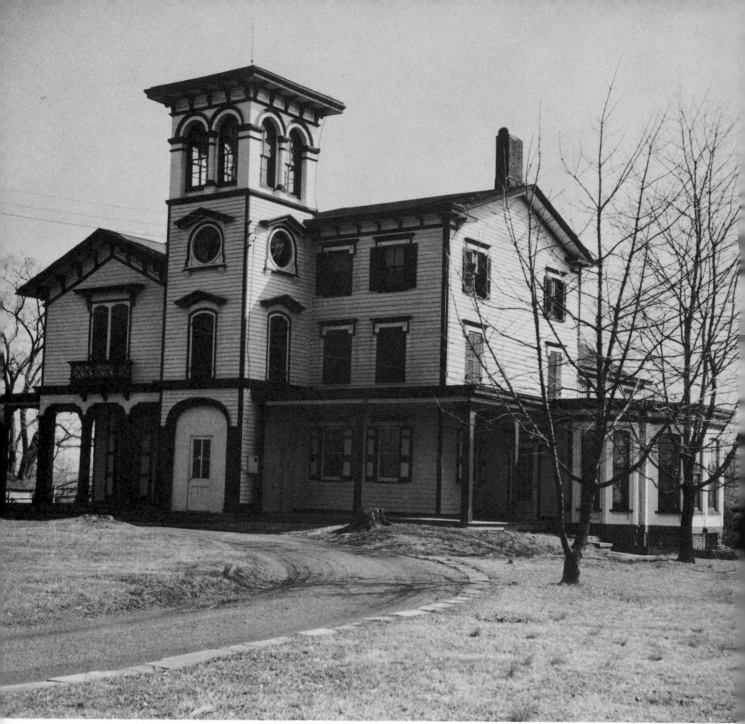

The Italian stone villa style was often translated into wood. Purists sputter with rage about this sort of thing but it really does no harm when the result is as pleasant as this white-and-green clapboard home at Flemington, N.J.

104

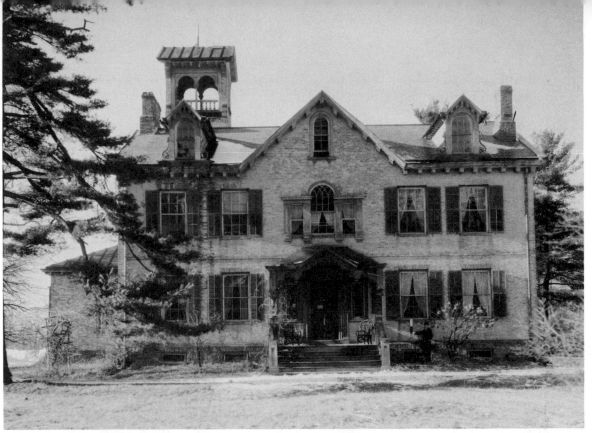

President Martin Van Buren was described as "a little, dapper gentleman, elegant and refined, the pink of fashion and politeness." He had Lindenwald, his old homestead at Kinderhook, New York, remodeled into a fashionable Italian villa; so here we have an eighteenth century home disguised as a nineteenth century house.

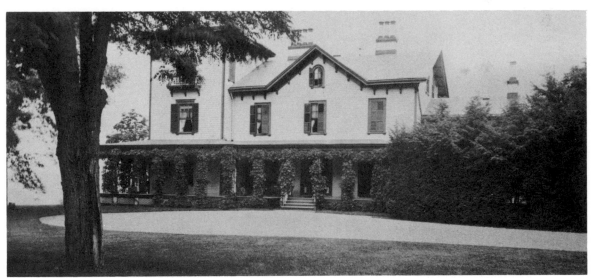

Millions of people have visited this house but few will recognize it from the picture. This is Springwood, the Roosevelt home at Hyde Park, New York, a fine example of Hudson River Bracketed. Since 1900 it has been hiding behind a Georgian front — a case of a nineteenth century building disguised in the twentieth century to look like an eighteenth century house.

Here are four examples to show how the prim-looking cube-shaped Italian villa with the lookout on top was Americanized:

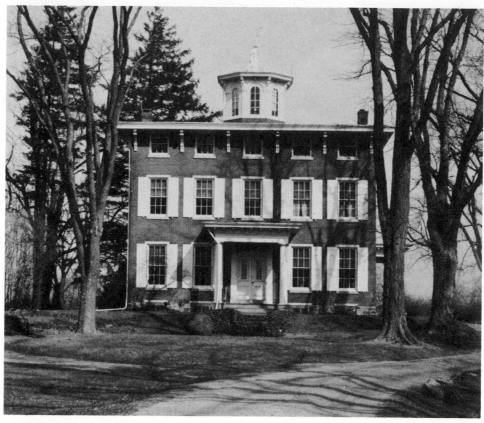

Red brick and white shutters at Marlton, New Jersey.

White clapboard, green shutters and fancy brackets at Mays Landing, New Jersey.

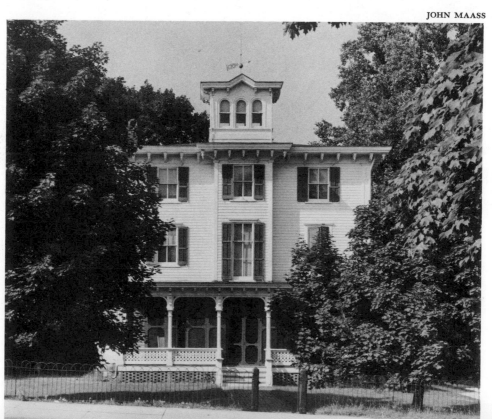

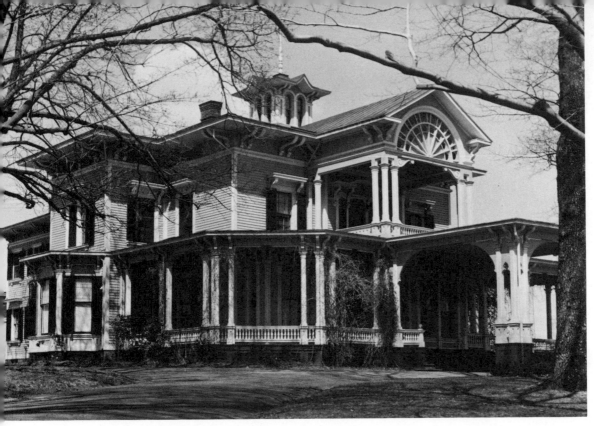

The cube has almost disappeared among the gay verandas of this Berlin, Connecticut, house.

This picture of Mr. T. J. Campau's residence in Detroit, Michigan, was described as "showing that he lives in a style becoming his wealth and position. His brick mansion was erected by himself in 1869 and is furnished in princely style." Note the matching coach house.

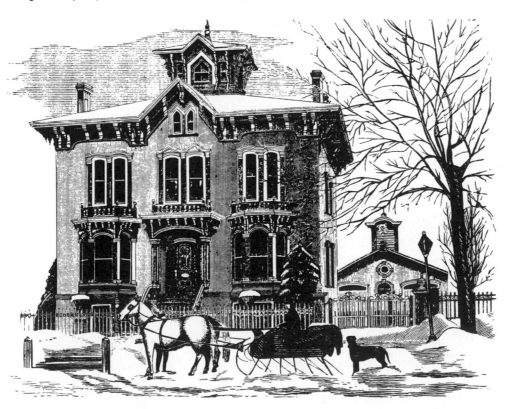

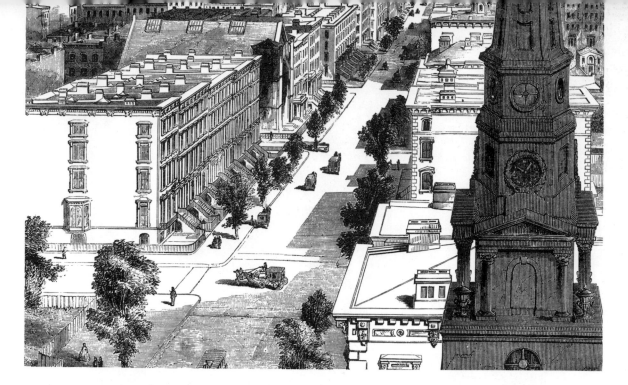

This 1857 view of New York's Fifth Avenue — looking south from 36th Street — shows blocks of Italianate town houses.

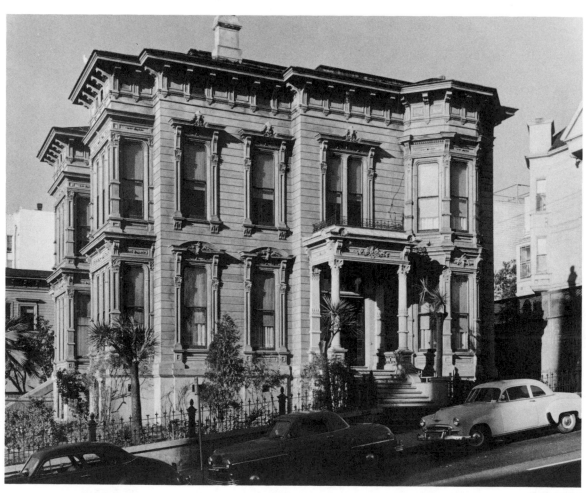

San Francisco has many houses with fanciful Renaissance details.

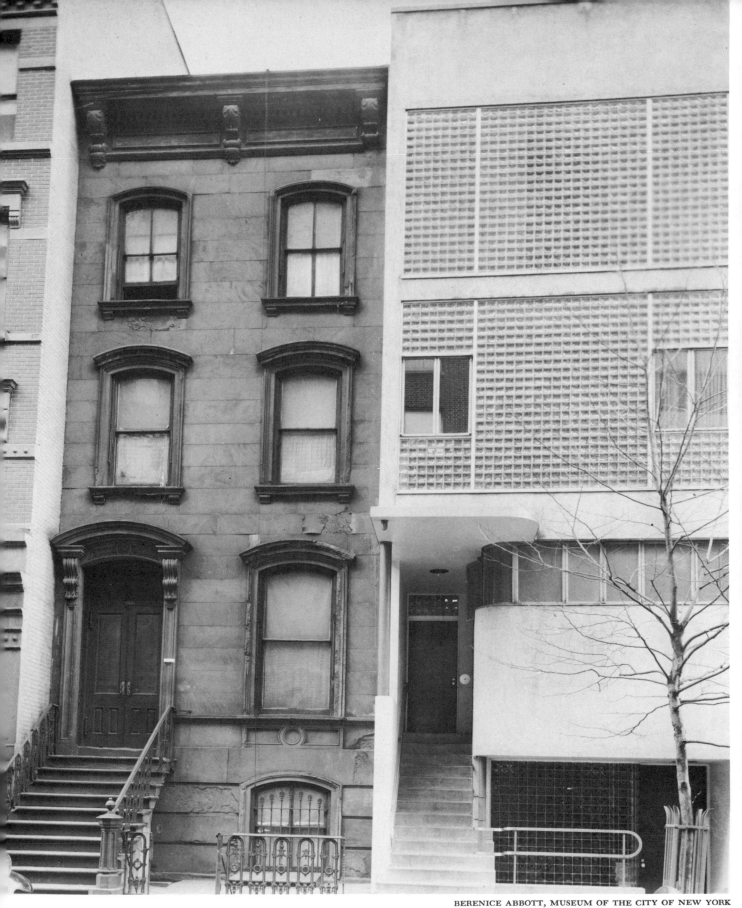

Two neighbors in Manhattan. Although the house on the right was modernized in the nineteen thirties by a distinguished contemporary architect, it now looks more dated than the brownstone next door.

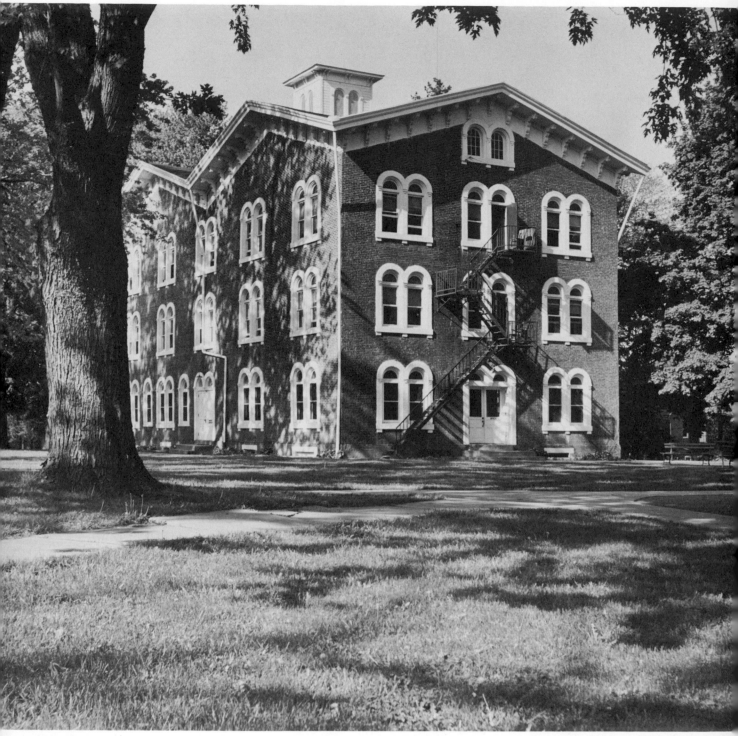

Selinsgrove Hall at Susquehanna University in Pennsylvania — a crisp, clean-cut design of red brick with white stone trim.

110

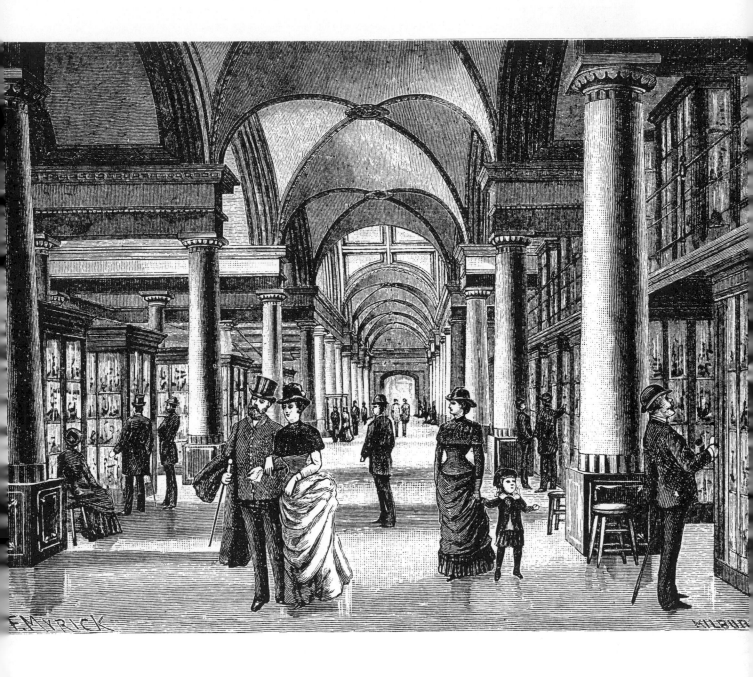

This surrealist scene is South Hall at the Patent Office, Washington, where "visitors are allowed to gratuitously inspect the vast collections of models."

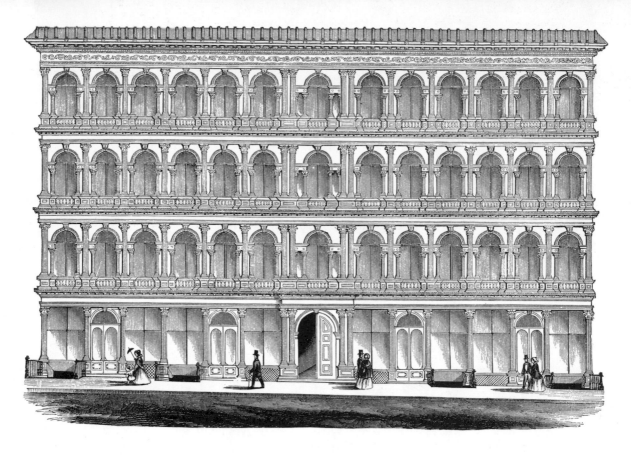

Mercantile palazzo prefabricated by the Badger Architectural Iron Works.

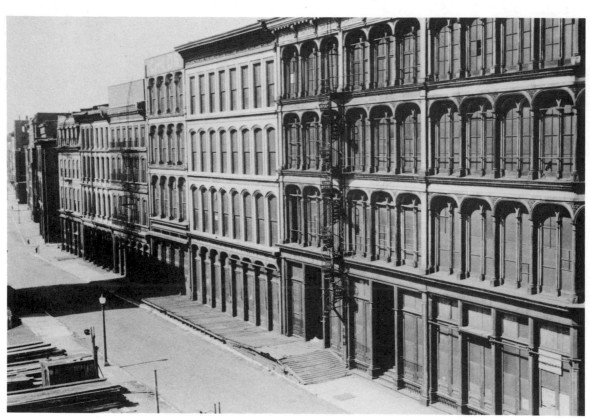

Commercial buildings on the Saint Louis riverfront; these were demolished in the nineteen forties.

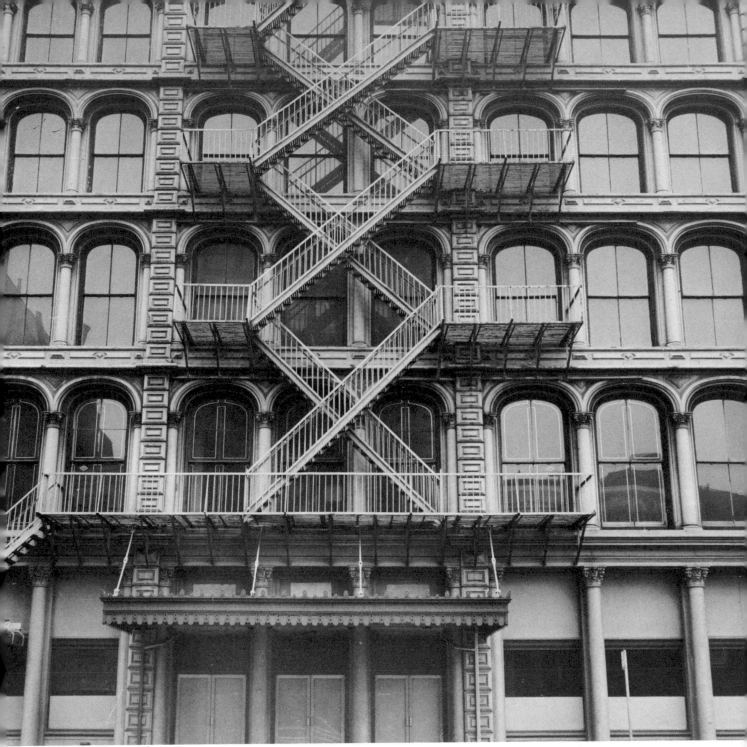

A. T. Stewart's "uptown" department store in New York was built in 1862; it later became the John Wanamaker store. Note the simplified design and the large glass area of this cast-iron façade. This photograph was taken in 1956, just before the abandoned building was destroyed by fire.

CHAPTER 5

THE MANSARDIC ERA

The French Roof is in great request. Public and private dwellings and even stables are covered with it and no man who wants a fashionable house, will be without it.

— SAMUEL SLOAN

The new "French Roof" was already over two hundred years old; it had been named after the celebrated architect François Mansart who died in 1666. A mansard roof has four steep sides broken by large dormer windows. This elegant form grew out of a quite workaday function — it had originally been designed to provide more headroom and more light in the attic. The space under a peaked roof is a cramping triangular tunnel but the top floor of a mansarded house is fit to live in.

The mansard's striking silhouette soon became a hallmark of fine French homes and chateaux, it enjoyed a great revival during the short-lived Second Empire. Napoleon III ordered a grandiose rebuilding program for his capital city and the Emperor's chief planner, Baron Haussmann, crisscrossed Paris with wide boulevards and avenues; these were bordered by tall, mansarded apartment houses. Great new wings in an ornate Neo-Renaissance style rose to link the ancient Louvre

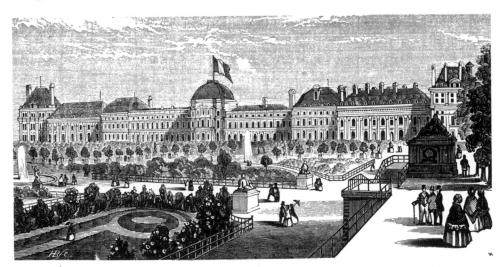

and Tuileries palaces. The glittering Paris of Napoleon and Eugenie was the world's center of elegance and progress, the scene of two successful International Expositions in 1855 and 1867. Some Americans visited these World's Fairs and many more admired lithographs and

117

engravings of the new Paris and its splendid architecture at home.* The mansard crossed the Atlantic in the late eighteen fifties and scored a smashing success. It cannot be traced to any French immigrant or Paris-trained American architect. French-roofed houses were also built in England, Germany, Italy, Latin America and other countries outside France but the triumph of the mansard in the United States was on a far larger scale. We can give no better explanation than to say simply that Americans liked this powerful, exuberant kind of design very much. It suited a vigorous, expanding nation. It must again be pointed out that France provided only the first spark, American mansard is distinctly American and not an imitation of Parisian models.

The mansard style reigned supreme until the middle seventies when it went out of fashion as suddenly as it had appeared. After 1876 most public buildings were done in the grim "Romanesque" of Richardson and his numerous imitators; the fussy "Queen Anne Style" was preferred for new homes. The Mansard Era was short but busy; the Civil War did not bring construction to a halt — on the contrary, the war set off a spectacular building boom.

There was no design problem which was not solved the mansard way during these years. The French roof covered home and school, bank and store, mill and factory, depot and firehouse, workhouse and poorhouse. Most church builders remained faithful to Victorian Gothic but the parsonage next door often sported a mansard.

American Mansard was considered the perfect style to express the dignity of government at every level. The United States Post Office, the state university, the county courthouse, the city hall and the township hall — all were crowned with mansarded roofs and often had towers with mansards of their own. For some years A. B. Mullett, supervising architect of the United States Treasury Department, held a virtual monopoly on the design of major Federal buildings**; he preferred

---

* Matthew Vassar owned a lithograph of the Tuileries Palace and proudly wrote on it, "Similar to Vassar College." This first college for women in America was also the first one — for either sex — to occupy a building of mansard design.

**Mullett was a power in the Republican Party; in 1874 he had a fisticuffs encounter in the streets of Cincinnati with a local politician named Henry Kessler. The Cincinnati *Enquirer* commented: "Mullett is a man of genius. He put a beautiful architectural adornment on Kessler yesterday."

the French Renaissance manner with row upon row of pillars and columns. The mansard roof itself took many shapes, its slope could be straight, or concave, or convex, or both combined in an S-curve. The dormer windows might be rectangular or pointed and gabled or round like portholes. Some large roofs even featured a double row of dormers, one above the other.

The great hotels of the seventies displayed American Mansard at its most splendiferous. Many of them are gone now. The San Francisco Palace with its marble-paved, glass-roofed Grand Court and seven stories of sun-catching bay windows did not survive the Great Earthquake and Fire. The showplaces of Saratoga Springs, the United States Hotel and The Grand Union, were both demolished in the nineteen fifties after they had ceased to show a profit. Many attractive smaller hotels with inviting piazzas and mansard roofs are still in service. Merchants, bankers and insurance companies built mansardic headquarters, visible proof of solid prosperity. Many of these mercantile palaces have been replaced by skyscrapers but some survive in older business districts like Lower Manhattan.

The mansard proved wonderfully adaptable to American homes — in the city, in the suburb, in the town, in the village and on the farm. American Mansard homes stand alone, semi-detached or in the row of a city block. They were built of wood, red brick, yellow brick, marble, granite, limestone, slate, sandstone, fieldstone, brownstone, serpentine stone. They could be stuccoed, painted, clapboarded, shingled. They may be white, yellow, orange, red, buff, brown, gray, green, blue or any two- or three-tone combination of these colors. They are plain as a box or fancy with gingerbread, ironwork, moldings, quoins, brackets and colored glass. The style has become identified in the folklore of America with the mansions of the rich, especially the newly rich, but this has little basis in fact. For every pretentious mansard residence there are hundreds of middling-size homes with the French roof. Obviously a mansarded house cannot have less than two stories, most of them have three which was just about the right size for the large Victorian family. All this made for a most pleasant diversity within unity of style.

Yet the houses of this period have been hit by doctrinaire criticism

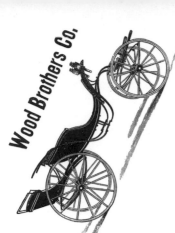

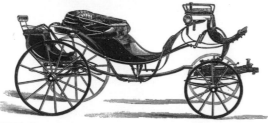

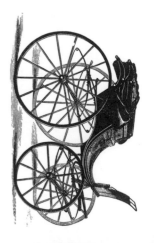

Wood Brothers Co.,

CARRIAGE MANUFACTURERS,

740 Broadway, N. Y.

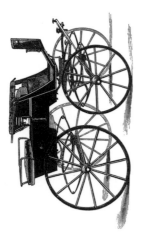

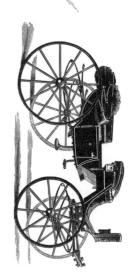

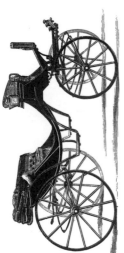

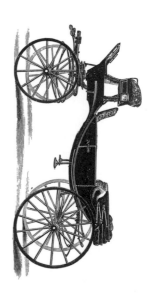

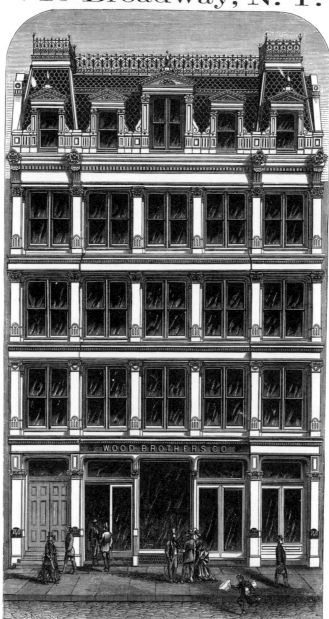

Constantly in Stock, and in course of Construction, all the **POPULAR STYLES OF PLEASURE CARRIAGES**, from the Newest Original and Selected Designs. All Goods warranted, and **UNSURPASSED** for **BEAUTY** and **EXCELLENCE**.

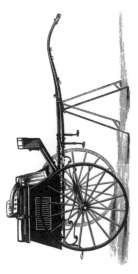

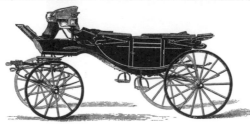

of unequaled ferocity. They were built in Mark Twain's "Gilded Age" and critics have called it an architectural "Parvenu Period" or "Age of Horror." The following adjectives from the Dictionary of Academic Invective have been applied freely: monstrous, atrocious, barbarous, imbecilic, degraded, meretricious, debased, corrupt and especially "immoral."* Why such raging against mere man-made objects? Because the critics were taught to despise the men who made the buildings. Mansarded houses are often described as being in the "General Grant Style." Here is a clear case of guilt by association with an administration which has long had a Bad Press. U. S. Grant himself lived in a pleasant red brick house with white woodwork and a *flat* roof.

The typical mansard house is handsome without and comfortable within. The best of them with their deep porches, tall French windows, massive cornices and sweeping roofs topped by iron cresting are buildings of striking power and dignity.

There is always room for disagreement in matters of architectural taste. Some contemporary buildings are admired for their pure and pristine design while detractors profess to find them arid and sterile. Only a thin line divides the "bold and self-confident" from the "vulgar and ostentatious" and we have of course never given the Victorians the benefit of the doubt. You are invited to do so now and the pictures are offered in evidence.

* Lewis Mumford who has both learning and wit called the mansard roof itself "a crowning indignity" and coined the delightful term "Uglified Renaissance."

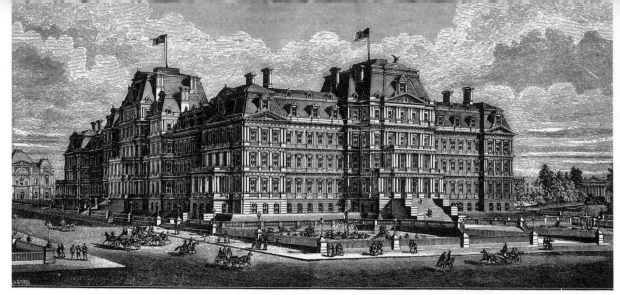

THE STATE, WAR, AND NAVY BUILDING.

A. B. Mullett's $12,000,000 design was described as "an almost perfect specimen of architecture . . . the interior has been constructed in a very magnificent and yet entirely substantial manner." As the Federal Government grew, the War and Navy departments moved to buildings of their own, the State Department remained here until after World War II; "Old State" now houses the President's Executive Offices. The White House and the Treasury Building are seen on the right; the "French Style" building in the left background is the Corcoran Gallery of Art, now the U. S. Court of Claims.

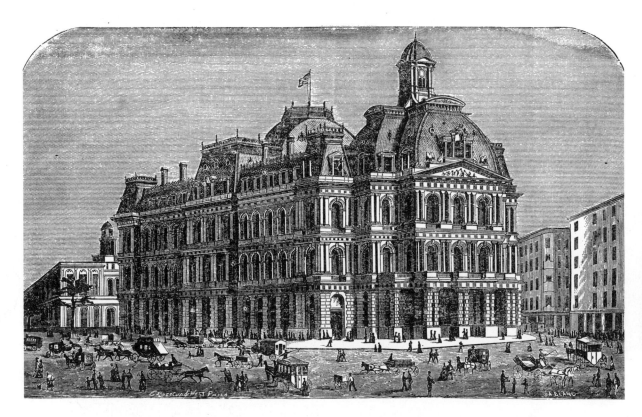

The same architect also built the post offices in New York, Boston and Philadelphia. The New York office on a wedge-shaped lot next to City Hall had bulging domes both fore and aft. All three of these pompous buildings have been demolished and replaced by bland "Neo-Classic" structures.

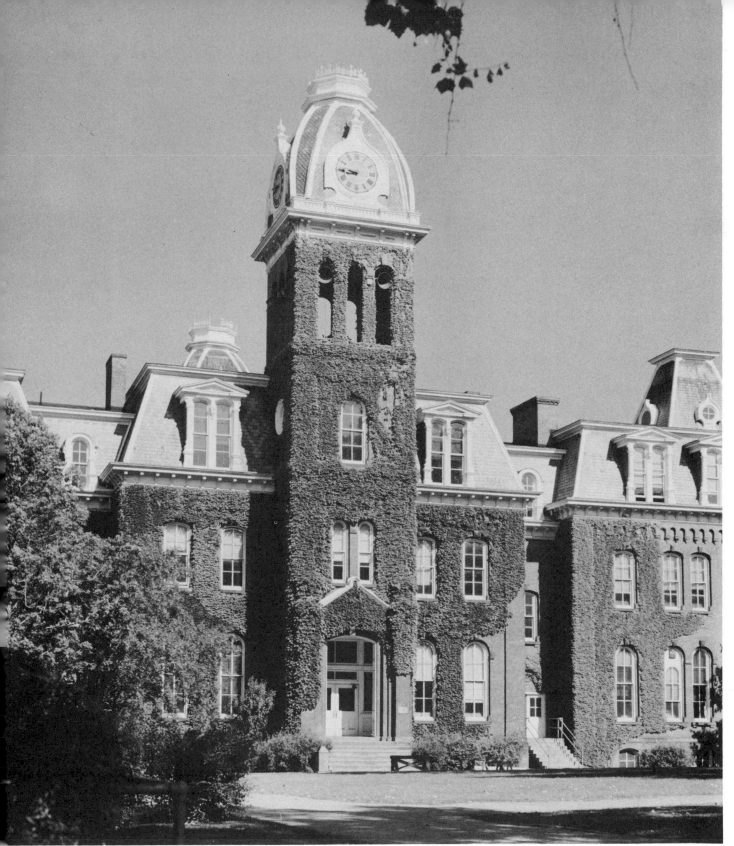

Dozens of colleges and universities were founded in the decade after the Civil War. This is why there are so many dear "Old Main" buildings with mansard roofs and clock towers on campuses all over the country. The example above is Woodburn Hall at West Virginia University, Morgantown.

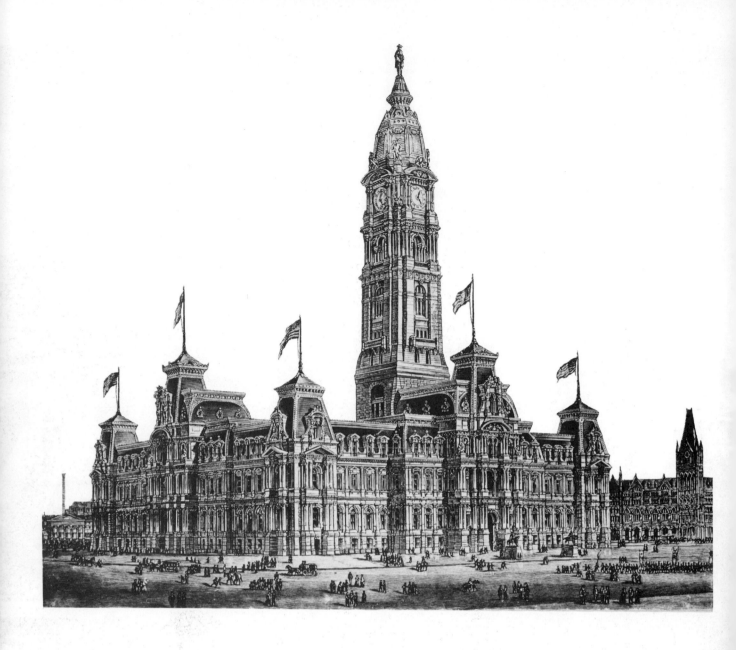

Philadelphia's City Hall is American Victorian at its most spectacular. This building is obviously not in good taste but it has something more important — CHARACTER. The Hall took ten years to build, twenty more to decorate, the cost was over $24,000,000. There are fourteen and a half acres of floor space and a 548-foot tower. What appears to be a little figure at the top of the tower is a statue of William Penn, 37 feet high and weighing 53,000 pounds. It is the work of the sculptor Alexander Calder; his grandson and namesake is now famous as the creator of the airy "mobiles" — a neat example of changing fashions in American art.

124

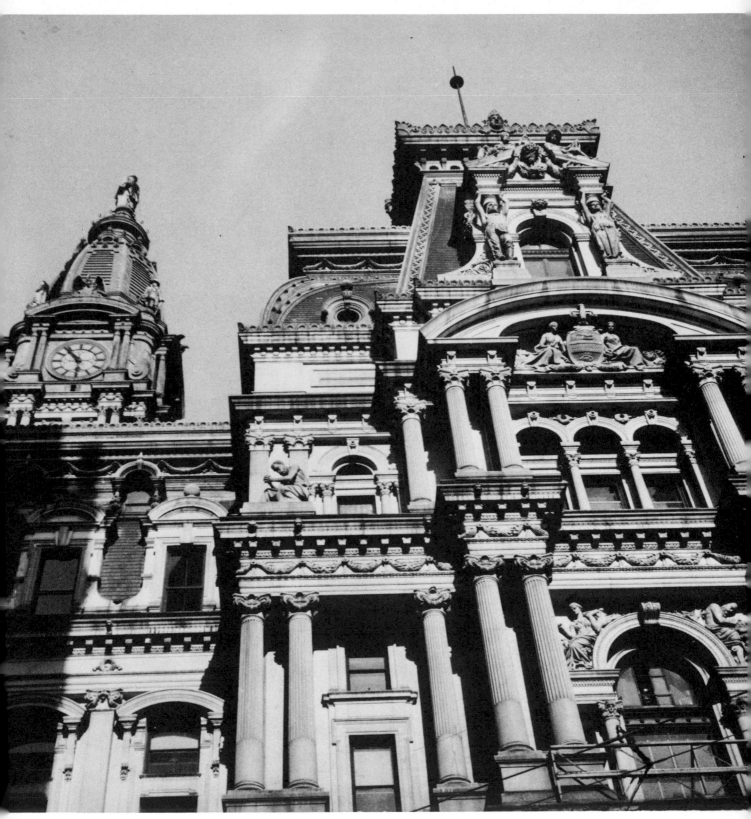

125

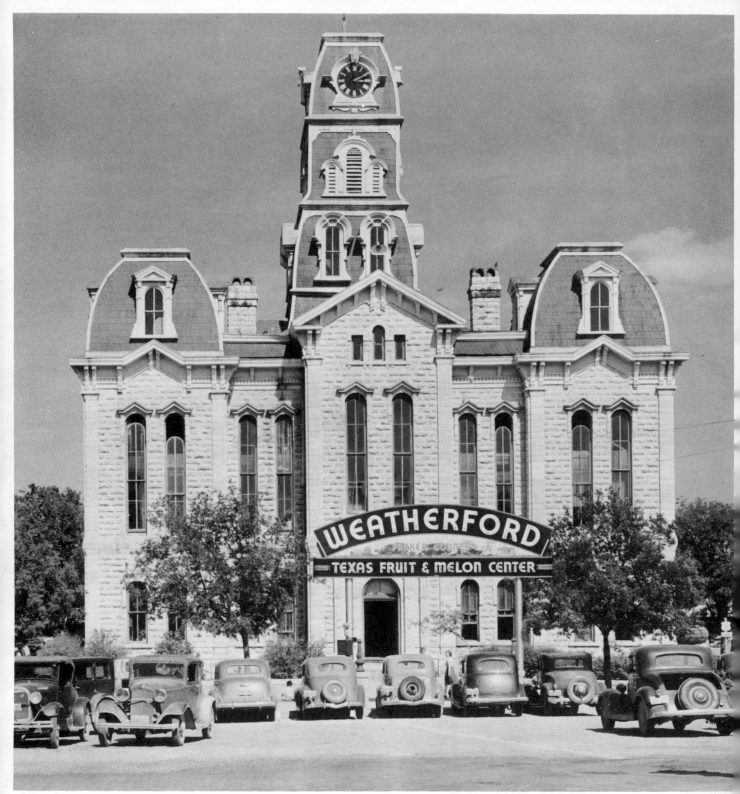

The mansarded county courthouse is a familiar type. Here is a cheerfully exaggerated Texas specimen.

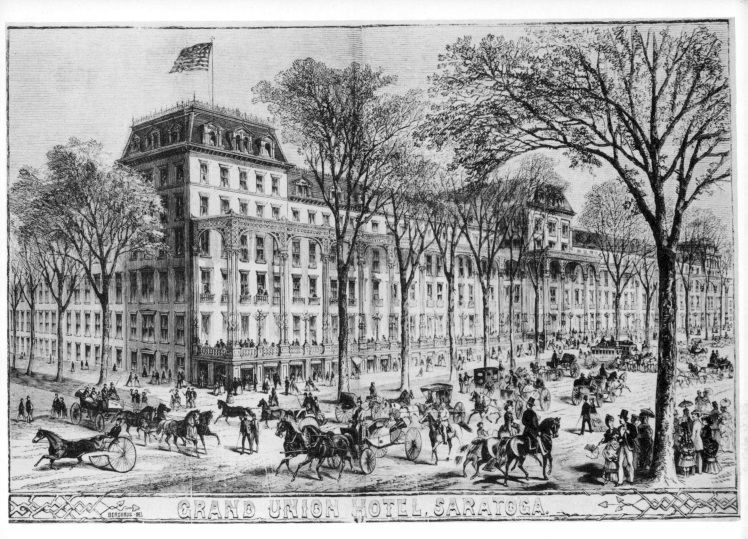

GRAND UNION HOTEL, SARATOGA.

In 1873 the Grand Union advertised: "This famous Hotel is now open for the season, refitted and improved throughout. No expense has been spared to make it the most comfortable and elegant, as well as the coolest, Hotel at Saratoga Springs. The Bath-Rooms and Water-Closets — heretofore objectionable — have been entirely removed; and instead, they have been placed in convenient parts of the Hotel, trimmed with Black Walnut and Maple. The immense Dining Hall — two hundred feet by fifty-five — as also the extensive range of parlors, have been fitted with Crystal Chandeliers and Reflectors, and the famous Ball-Room, with three Crystal Sunlights, will produce a brilliancy of effect that can be more easily imagined than expressed."

JOHN MAASS

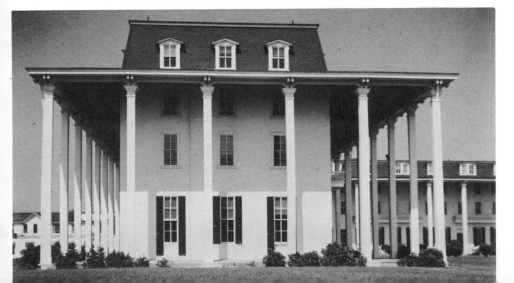

Congress Hall Hotel at Cape May, New Jersey, is not unusually large but the tall piazza gives it an air of real grandeur.

Model Residence for a Physician.

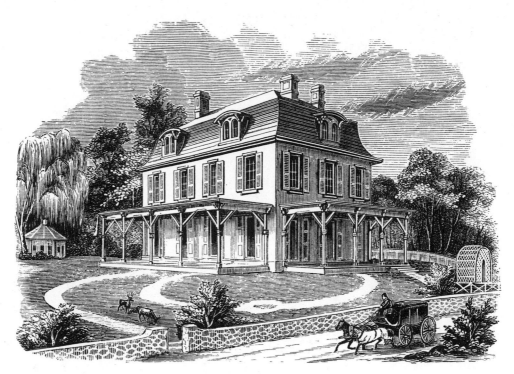

An early mansarded home. The architect reports: "The estimate for this design, in the vicinity of West Chester, was $3,000; but we think it was probably built for a little less under the careful management of the proprietor."

A Guide to Vermont states: "There were fewer great fortunes amassed here during the latter half of the Nineteenth Century and consequently fewer baroque mansions of the General Grant 'Gingerbread' manner. Occasionally one may be seen however with wide lawns and weathervaned coachhouse, dominating a village in ornate ugliness." Here is one of these "ugly" Vermont houses.

JOHN MAASS

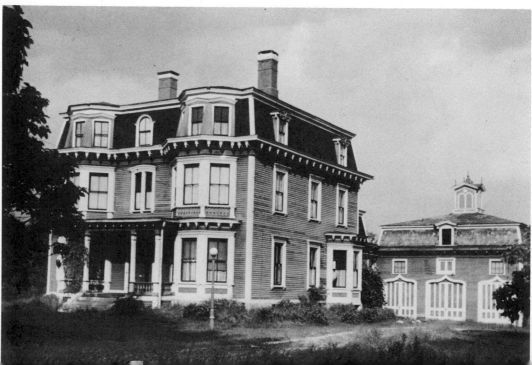

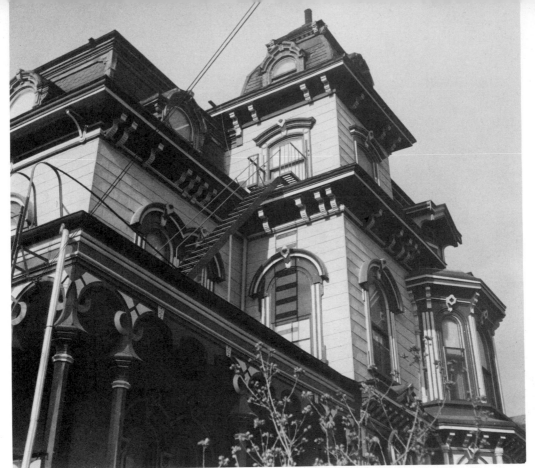

Two houses on the same street in Elizabeth, New Jersey, display the mansard manner's endless variety. The one above sports a dazzling color scheme — mint green walls, dark green and golden yellow trim, shocking pink roof.

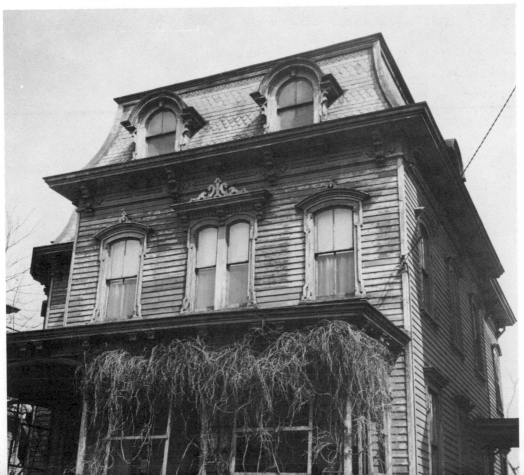

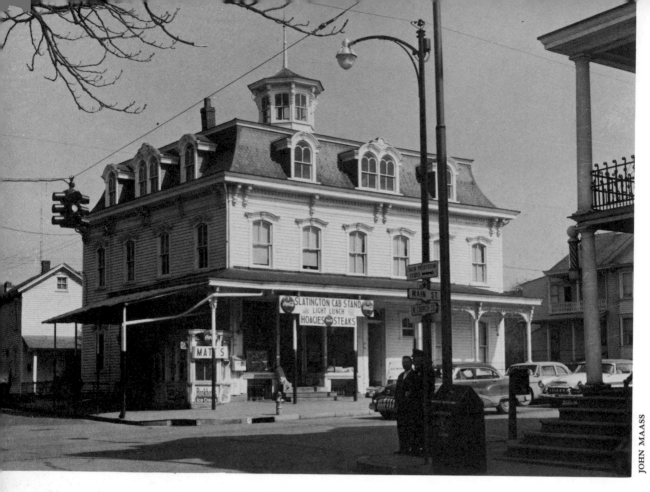

Are mansard buildings really gloomy? Main Street of Slatington, Pennsylvania; side porch of a Brewster, New York, home.

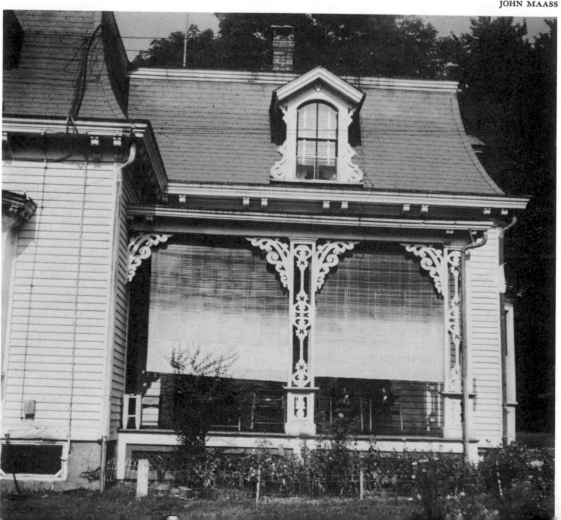

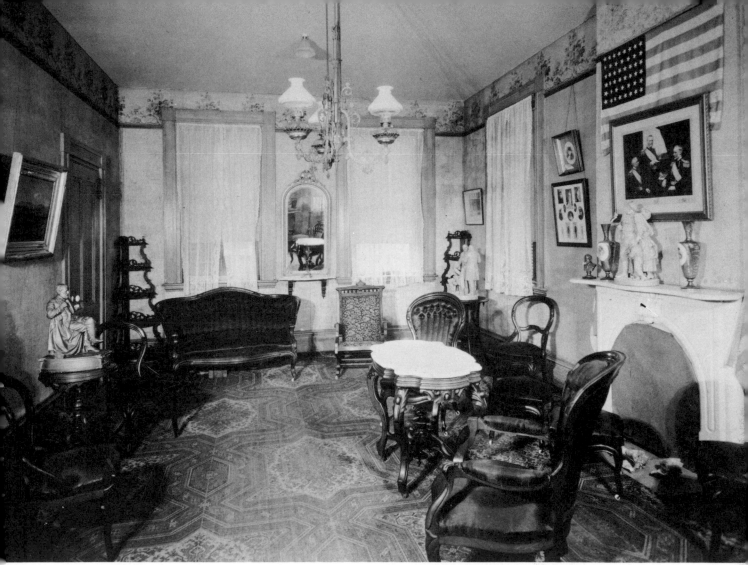

The authentic "General Grant Style" of interior decoration. This is the parlor of the Galena, Illinois, home where General and Mrs. U. S. Grant lived between the War and the Presidency. Note the three plaster sculptures.

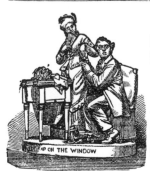

ROGERS'
STATUARY.

The Tap on the Window.

A new group, price $15.

Enclose 10c. for catalogue and prints to
JOHN ROGERS,
212 Fifth Avenue, cor.
26th Street,
NEW YORK

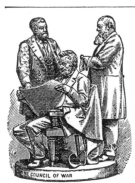

THE
COUNCIL OF WAR,
A group of statuary by John Rogers, representing Lincoln, Grant, and Stanton examining a map of the campaign. Price $25 00.

This and other groups will be delivered at any railroad station in the United States, free of expense, on receipt of the price. Send for Illustrated Catalogue and Price-List to
JOHN ROGERS,
212 Fifth Ave., N. Y.

John Rogers was the most successful sculptor of all times. He sold over 100,000 of his casts. The homey, realistic, sentimental "Rogers Groups" are the most characteristic of American Victoriana. After fifty years of disrepute they are now again valued and collected.

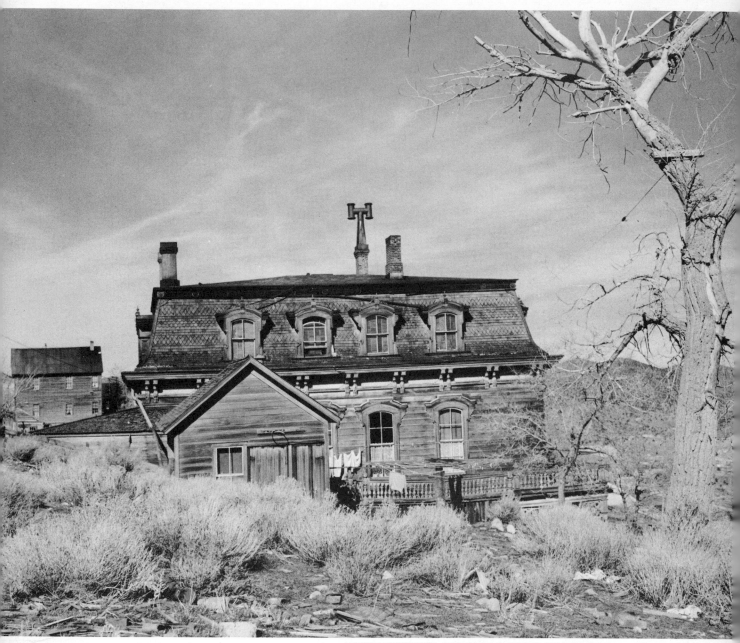

The Mansard in the Far West:

The old Clinton Mining Company office at Virginia City, Nevada, dates from the silver mining boom of the sixties.

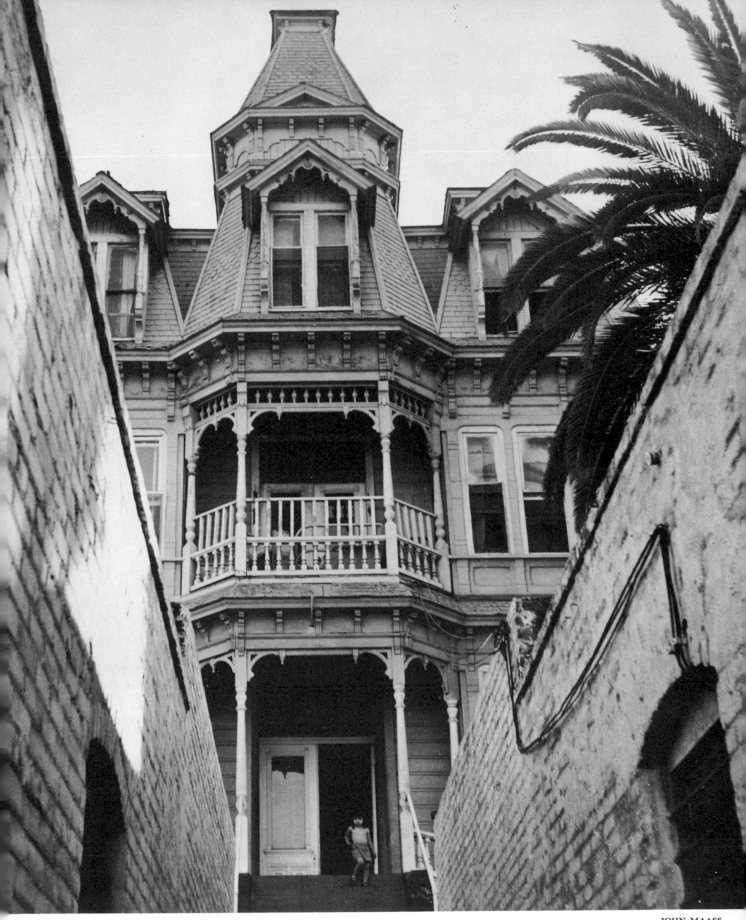

Many steps lead up to this bright green apartment house on Temple Street,
Los Angeles.

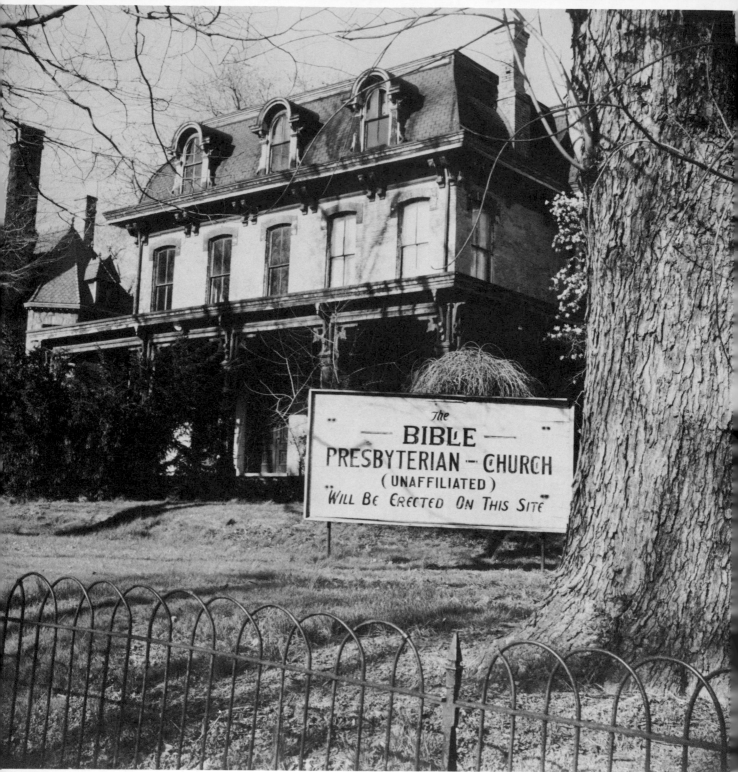

The mansard houses are being torn down by the thousands; Chester, Pa.

CHAPTER 6

UNEXPLORED TERRITORY

. . . carpenters and builders . . .

—2 CHRONICLES 34:11

In 1846 Henry Howe, a dark-haired young man of thirty, saddled his white horse and set out on a tour of Ohio. In every town from Ashtabula to Zanesville he recorded local history and drew neat sketches; he published all this information under the title *Historical Collections of Ohio*. It enjoyed great and well-deserved success*; Rutherford B. Hayes, later President of the United States, wore out ten copies of the book. Forty years later, Howe — now a patriarch with flowing white beard — decided to repeat his tour; the journey turned into a triumphal procession for the beloved author. In the foreword to a new edition he wrote: "Everywhere I made arrangements with local photographers and took them to the standpoints I selected for views to be taken. They were for new engravings to make a pictorial contrast of the Ohio of 1846 and that of 1886. About one hundred were seen."

The earlier views were mostly sleepy village scenes; the dusty road runs between plain, low buildings; in every county seat stands a little foursquare courthouse of identical design. The later views display a great variety of public and commercial architecture; the fancy new courthouse overlooks a public park; a hotel has taken the place of the old village inn; telegraph poles are much in evidence on the paved streets.

Howe's "before and after" pictures demonstrate that there was probably more change in American towns between 1846 and 1886 than there has been in the seventy years since. Today's Midwestern Main Street looks very much like Howe's later views: In the business section, the same old Victorian façades rise above the first floor clutter of be-chromed marquees and chain-store fronts, about the same number of cars are jammed up against the parking meters as there were buggies tied to the hitching posts.

* The book was not only packed with facts but presented hundreds of colorful stories like The Black Swamp Mutiny, The Coon-skin Library, The Bower of the Lost Child, The Guernsey County Meteor, Burning a Bewitched Horse, The Double Headed Baby, The Blue Rock Mine Disaster, Building a Navy in the Wilderness, Girls Stolen by Indians, Squire Brown and the Slave Hunters, An Ohio Robinson Crusoe, The Four Spies, The Sycamore of Fifteen Horsemen.

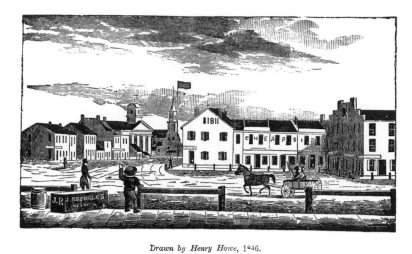

Drawn by Henry Howe, 1846.

PUBLIC SQUARE, URBANA.

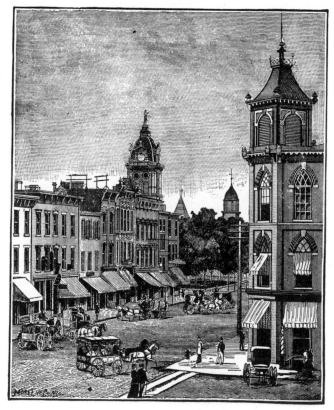

F. T. Graham, Photo., Urbana, 1886.

PUBLIC SQUARE, URBANA.

[Both views were taken from the same point. In the old view the building with the figures 1811 occupies the same site as that of the building with a tower on the right in the new view.]

138

UNEXPLORED TERRITORY

In most parts of the country, United States townscape is essentially Victorian. Main streets of mid-nineteenth century design and character far outnumber the carefully preserved relics from earlier periods. In the larger cities, the Victorian pattern may be obscured but in thousands of towns it is still clear.

Let's enter "Victoria, U.S.A.," a county seat, Population 8,000. (DRIVE CAREFULLY, WE LOVE OUR CHILDREN!, THE CHURCHES OF VICTORIA WELCOME YOU.) Elm trees along the sidewalk and thirty feet of front lawn before the frame houses. Main Street widens out into a public square, eight-sided bandstand in the center. Mansarded county courthouse with cast-iron Civil War soldier in front. The Victoria Hotel across the square (ROTARY CLUB MEETS FRIDAY 1 P.M.), rocking chairs on the piazza and every floor shaded by wooden galleries. Fraternal lodge hall with roundheaded windows and iron letters I.O.O.F. on the façade. First National Bank with the founding year 1871 boldly carved into the cornice. Down by the dammed river the long, red plant of the Victoria Woolen Mills stands empty (180,000 SQUARE FEET OF INDUSTRIAL SPACE FOR SALE OR RENT). The biggest mansion in town with cupola and honeysuckle-pattern iron verandas is now the Victoria Post, American Legion. On the West Side, the campus of the Victoria State Teachers College (FOUNDED 1841 AS THE VICTORIA ACADEMY. A STATE NORMAL SCHOOL SINCE 1869). Founders Hall with its clock tower was long the school's only building; it now houses the administration.

Victoria's Victorian core is encased in a thickening shell of twentieth century growth: Treeless tracts of "Cape Cod" boxes and "split level" houses; two large factories of similar design with glass brick lobbies and strip windows — both manufacture a uniform product; one bears the sign VICTORIA PLANT, CONSOLIDATED PLASTICS INC., the other VICTORIA HIGH SCHOOL. Past the juke joints, the roller rink, the drive-in theatre and YOU ARE LEAVING VICTORIA, COME AGAIN — VICTORIA CHAMBER OF COMMERCE.

Nineteenth century Victoria, U.S.A., had no unity of architectural style but it was a pleasant and successful ensemble of warmth, color, dignity and good cheer, quite as good in its own way as Old World towns. The business blocks were remarkably well integrated; their storefronts did not clash with the nearby homes and the beautifully lettered signs enlivened Main Street's façades. Compare Victoria's middle class residential street with its counterparts of 1920 and 1950! The older block is enhanced by its finer stand of trees, but it is infinitely superior on every other count, too. Compare the solid, spacious homes with the later houses, mean, cramped, tricked out with shoddy veneers of Pseudo Tudor, Fake Colonial, Imitation Mission and Cheapjack Ranch Style.

The nineteenth century has been blamed for the confusion of the United States city and townscape, but the twentieth has been a worse offender. Gas stations, parking lots, diners, telephone poles, hideous billboards, garish marquees, glaring neon signs — all these are the disfiguring marks of our own crass time.

The nineteenth century pattern was more pleasing although the towns just grew without benefit of formal planning. Their rapid growth was made possible by an American Victorian invention, the balloon-frame system of construction. The traditional American way of building a wooden house was to construct a framework of heavy timbers, locked together by mortise, tenon and wooden pegs and sheathed with hand-sawn clapboards. It required much time and skilled carpentry. The balloon frame consisted of thin sticks, nailed together and covered with boarding from the lumber mill*. A couple of men who knew how to handle common tools — and nearly all nineteenth century Americans did know how — could put up a balloon-framed house in a few days. Balloon frame was a nickname; it was thought at first that these flimsy houses would fly away in the first strong wind but they turned out to be perfectly sturdy**.

Old-fashioned history books concentrated on kings and presidents, affairs of court and state, they were brief on the everyday life of ordi-

---

* The whole system was in turn made possible by the introduction of cheap, factory-made iron nails.

** They also stood up well to earthquakes. In California even apartment houses of several stories are built with wooden balloon frames today.

nary citizens. In the same way, conventional architectural history is top-heavy with descriptions of ceremonial buildings — churches, palaces, state capitols. Their design was judged against the standard of Old World prototypes, "correctness of detail" was demanded. Utilitarian buildings were hardly considered to be "architecture" at all.

So the tens of thousands of non-residential buildings by anonymous carpenter-builders are the least known examples of American Victorian design. They are also the best. This American popular architecture has innumerable regional and local variations; there is no common denominator beyond a characteristic boldness of form and color.

Consider for instance the range of buildings which are connected with farming: Barns have long been the favorite of Sunday painters and other city folk who have discovered the delights of the barn dance and the country auction. Others are less well known; a handbook of the eighties entitled *Barns and Outbuildings* gives plans and advice on how to build the following: general farm barns, cattle barns, stables, dairy barns, cattle shelters, sheep barns and sheds, poultry houses, piggeries, carriage houses, corncribs, icehouses, dairy houses, springhouses, granaries, smokehouses, doghouses, birdhouses, silos, root houses*.

Although there are thousands of railroad fans and fire buffs, very little attention has been paid to those two colorful architectural Americana — the depot and the firehouse.

The following pictures are presented as samples of American Vernacular Design, an unexplored field for scholars to investigate and laymen to enjoy.

* Many of these are mere names to the city-bred author of the book which you are now reading.

141

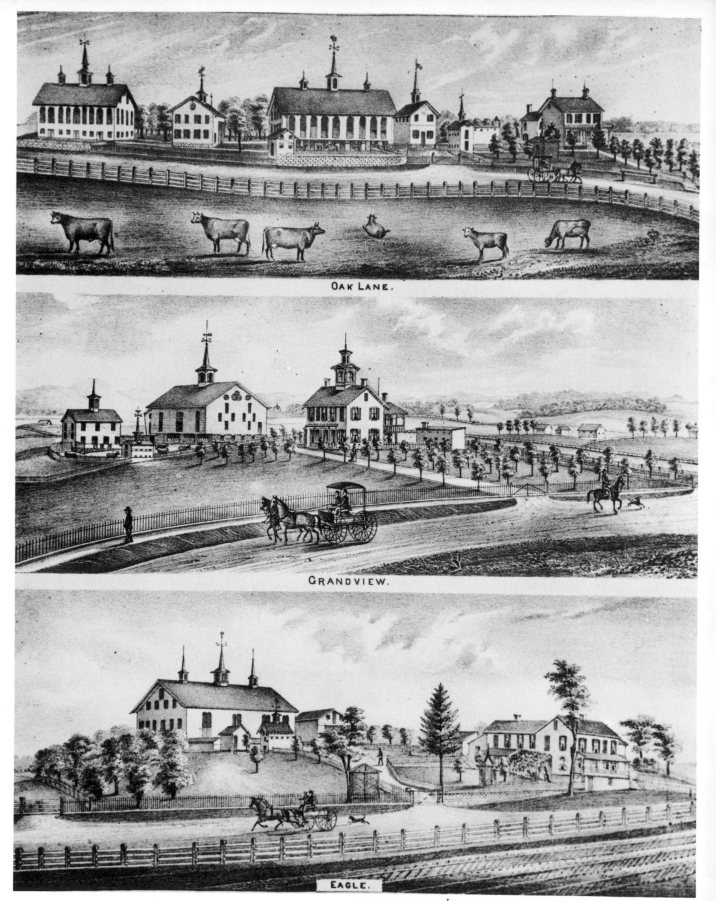

OAK LANE.

GRANDVIEW.

EAGLE.

EVERTS & STEWART'S ATLAS OF DAUPHIN COUNTY, PENNSYLVANIA (1875)

The barn is always the largest building on the farm and often more elaborate than the farmer's residence.

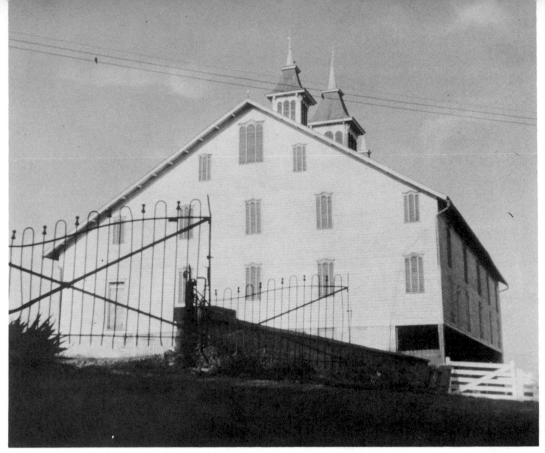

The height of barnyard elegance in Cumberland County, Pennsylvania — wrought-iron gate, stone foundation, clean white walls, bright green shutters, three ventilators with graceful red-roofed cupolas.

A fancy barn in Suffolk County, Long Island, New York.

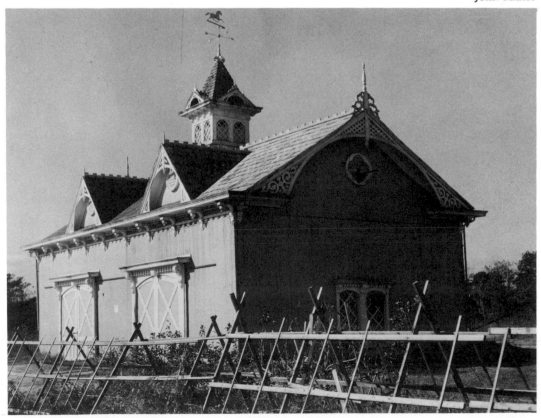

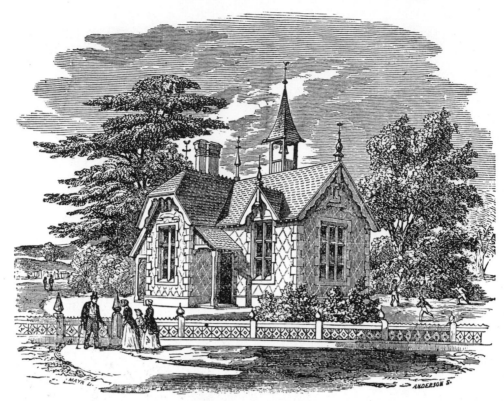

VILLAGE SCHOOL-HOUSE.

At present it is fashionable to sneer at the "one room schoolhouse" but Victorian schools were buildings of much charm and character. Thousands of them are still serving faithfully.

An abandoned "little red schoolhouse" in Berks County, Pennsylvania.

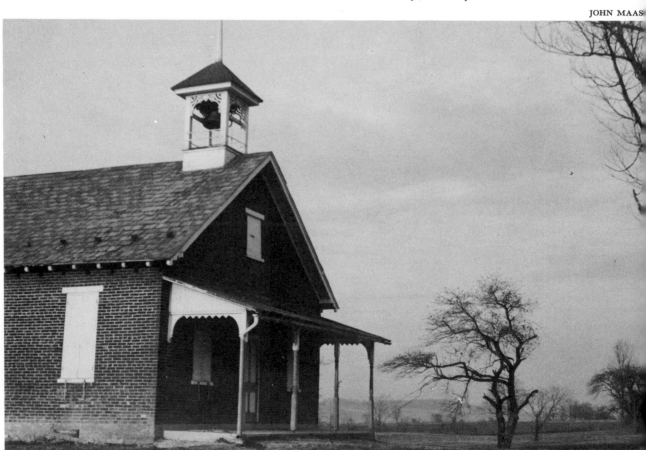

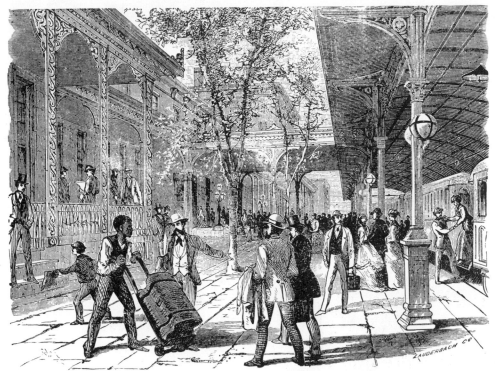

DEPOT OF THE PENNSYLVANIA RAILROAD AT ALTOONA.

Today the railroad station is often a backwater on the wrong side of town. In the nineteenth century it was the hub of the community, the link to the Great World — the wretched roads were blocked by snow and mud for months, good highways came only after the automobile. Railroading was the nineteenth century's premier industry, it offered the finest careers to ambitious men, the most jobs to skilled workers. The Victorian railroad depot was a place of glamour and excitement and designed to look the part.

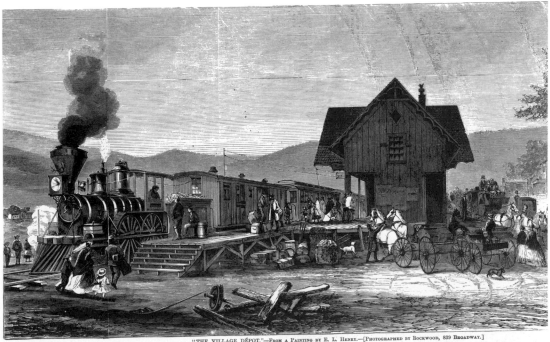

"THE VILLAGE DÉPOT."—FROM A PAINTING BY E. L. HENRY.—[PHOTOGRAPHED BY ROCKWOOD, 839 BROADWAY.]

The station at Stratford, Connecticut, served as the artist's model.

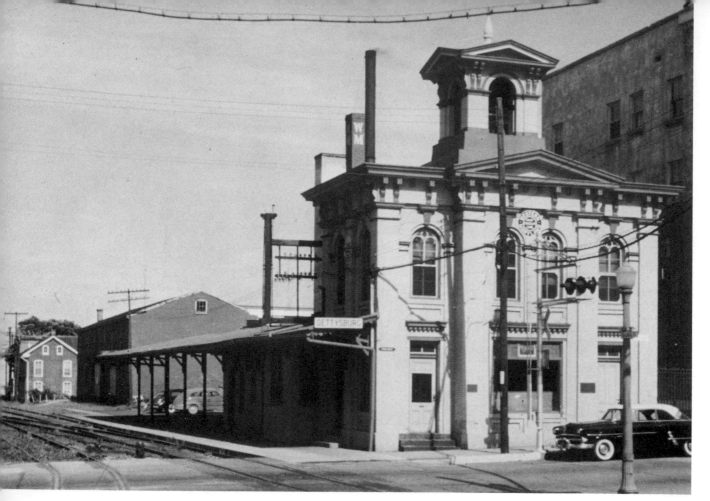

The beautiful Italianate style station of the old Hanover Junction and Gettysburg Line has light gray walls, scarlet trim and an elegant cupola for the bell. Trains arrived here the day after the battle to evacuate the wounded.

The footbridge over the tracks is another characteristic Victorian feature.

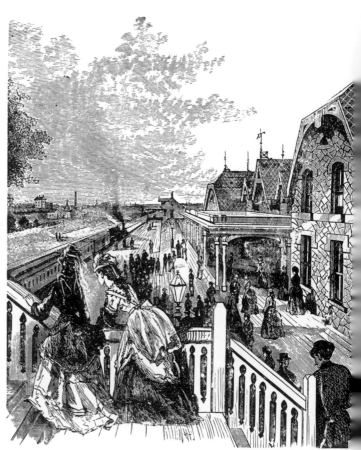

BRYN MAWR STATION, PENNSYLVANIA RAILROAD.

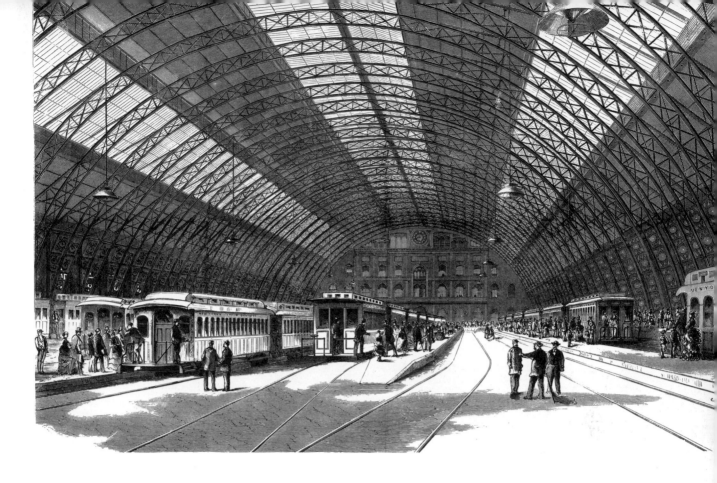

The huge iron train shed of Vanderbilt's old Grand Central Station in New York; built 1869-71 and demolished to make way for the present station.

Through these portals passed the people who took the Fulton Ferry from Brooklyn to Manhattan; a colossal statue of Robert Fulton in the central niche provided a final touch of splendor to this glittering façade.

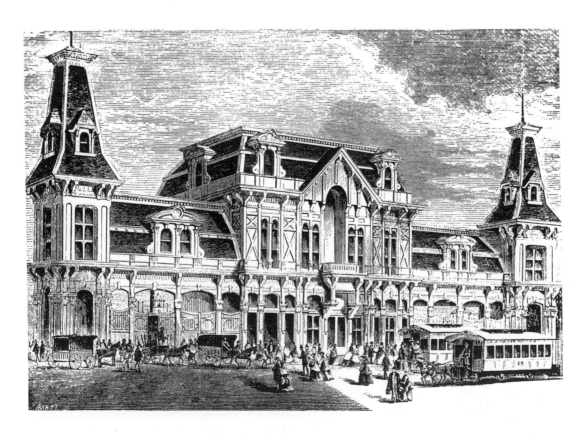

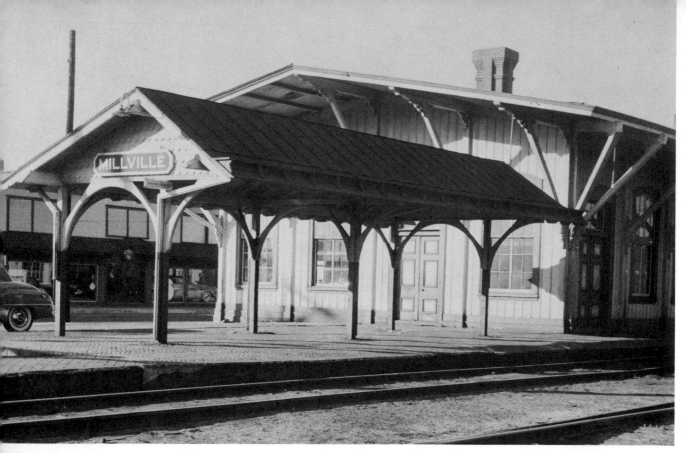

JOHN MAASS

The overhanging roof supported by large brackets is a hallmark of the "Railroad Style." It sheltered the passengers on the platform and had no pillars to get in the way of opening train doors.

CHARLES T. COINER

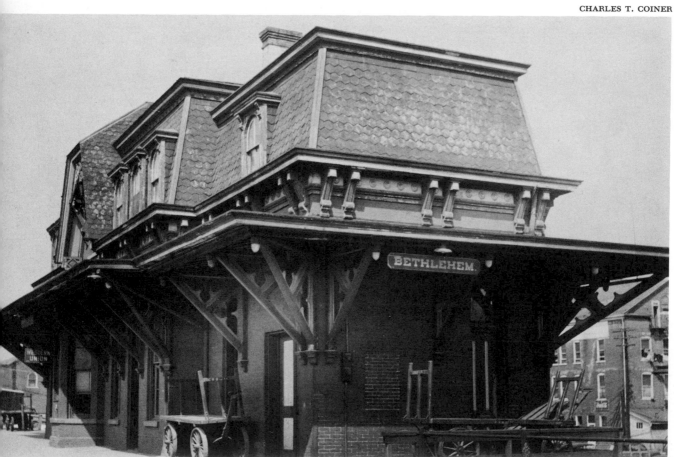

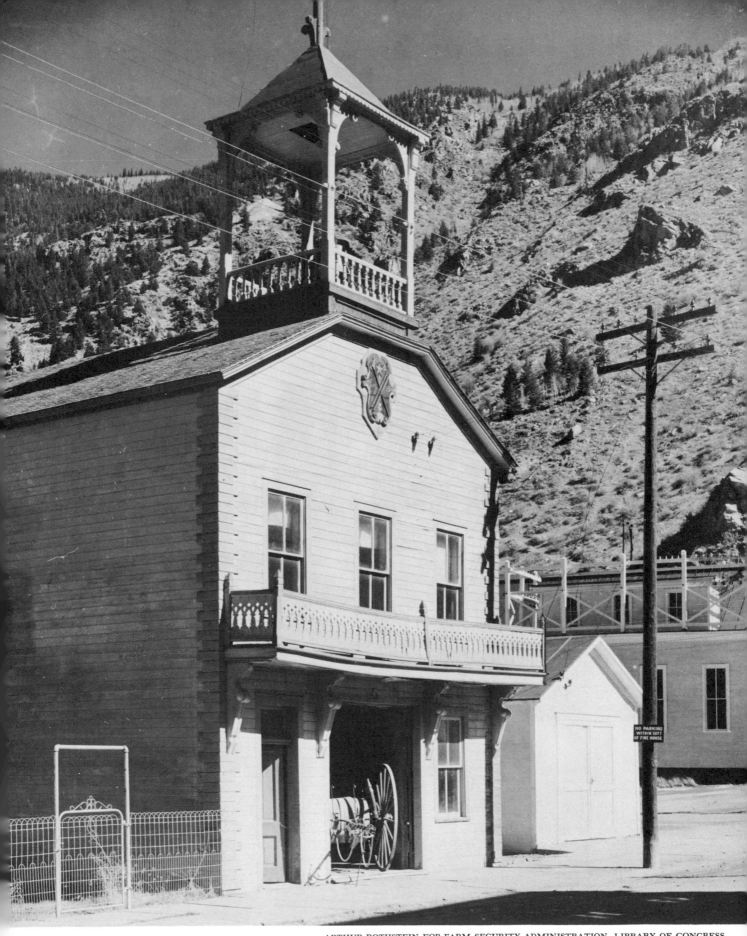

Firehouse at Georgetown, Colorado.

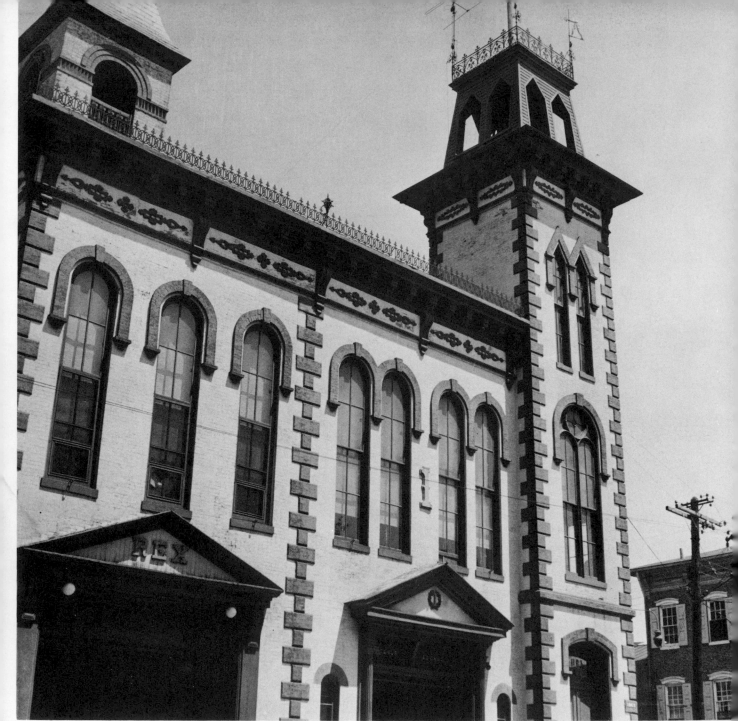

The flashy home of Laurel Engine Company and Rex Hook and Ladder Company of York, Pennsylvania, sports all the Victorian elegancies — white walls with chocolate-colored stone trim, Latin mottoes in gilt letters, iron laurel leaves and cresting, fancy bell tower and weather vane.

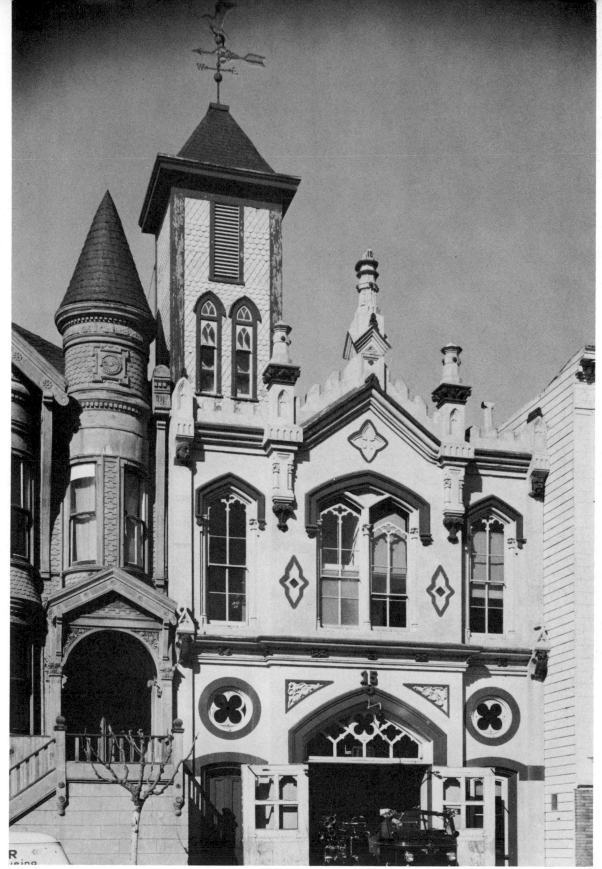

San Francisco's No. 15 Firehouse is a unique extravaganza from the eighteen eighties; it would make a perfect stage set for some Ruritanian operetta. The pinnacles are shaped like fireplugs and the gargoyles are really portraits of Fire Chiefs.

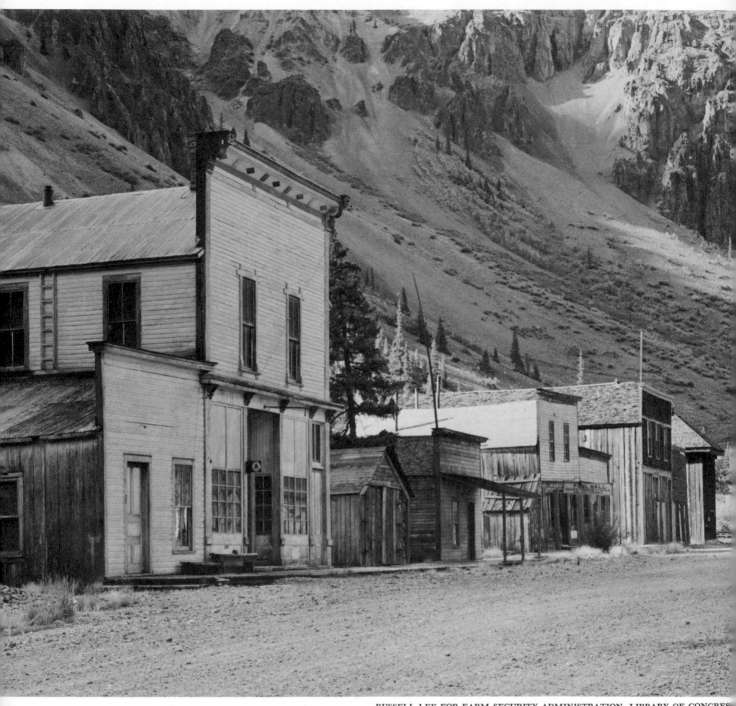

The Victorian buildings of Western ghost towns are a fantastic sight; this is the main street of Eureka, Colorado.

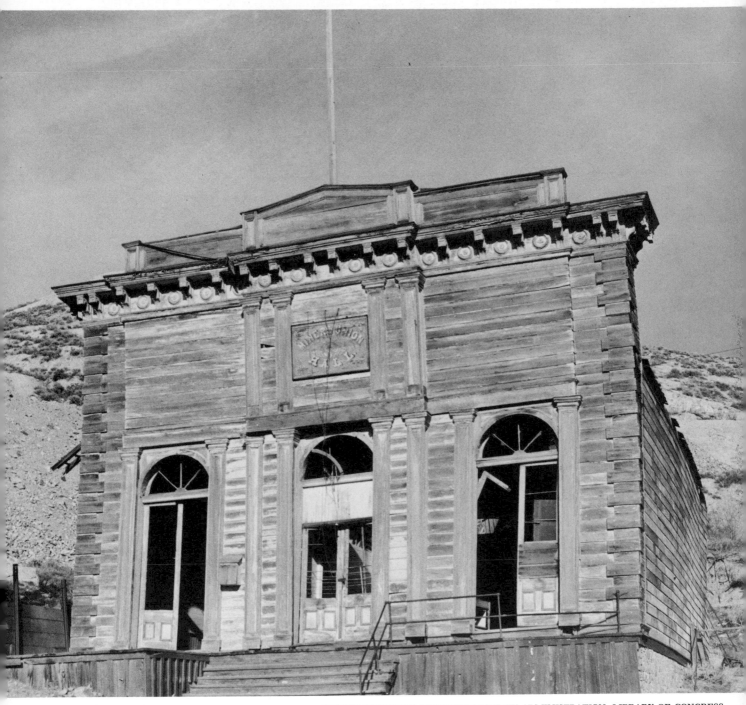

Miners Union Hall, Silver City, Nevada; this wooden false front imitates the effect of a stone façade.

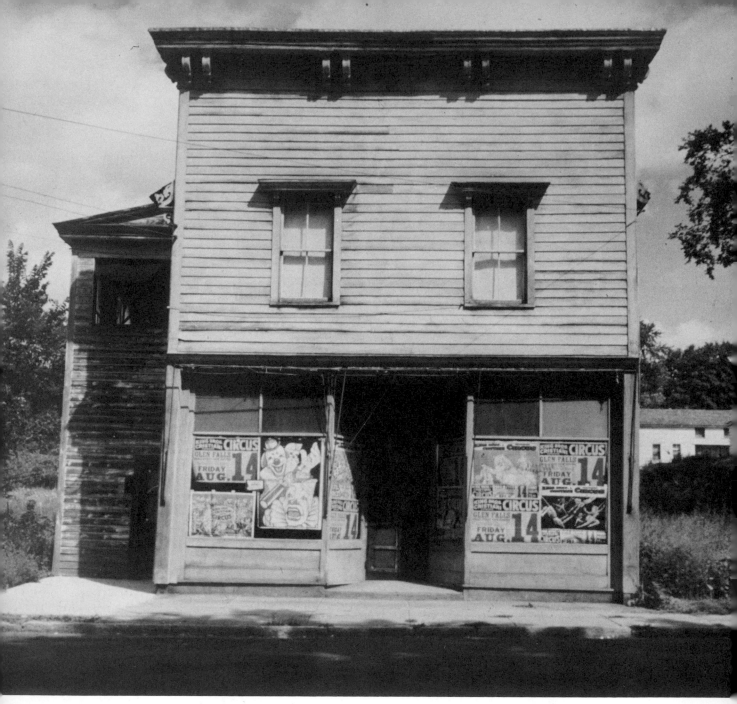

The famous false front made a shed look like a two-story building; it also provided a large surface for the merchant's sign. The false front is now regarded as a symbol of the West — the truth is exactly the other way around: The false fronts were built to give a citified "back home" look to a raw frontier town. They are common on Midwest Main Streets and an occasional example may still be seen in the East; a specimen at Hudson Falls, New York.

156

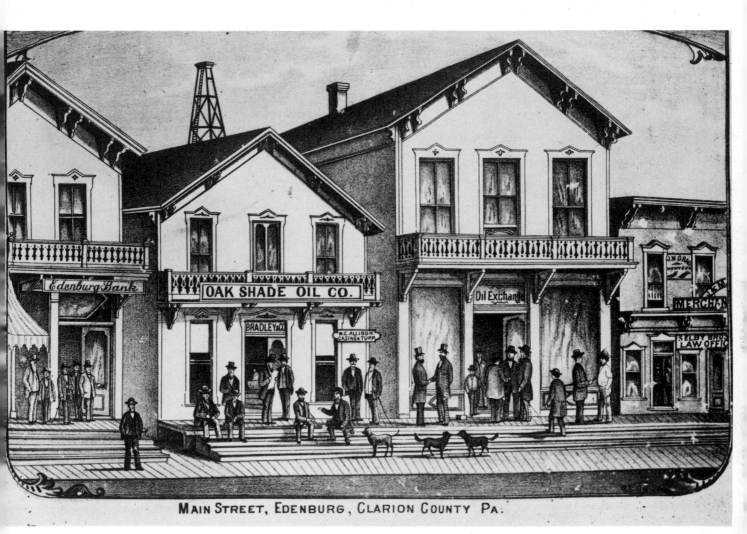

MAIN STREET, EDENBURG, CLARION COUNTY PA.

CALDWELL'S ATLAS OF CLARION COUNTY, PENNSYLVANIA (1877)

These hard-bitten pioneers are standing on the Main Street of an Eastern boom town in the Pennsylvania oil region.

157

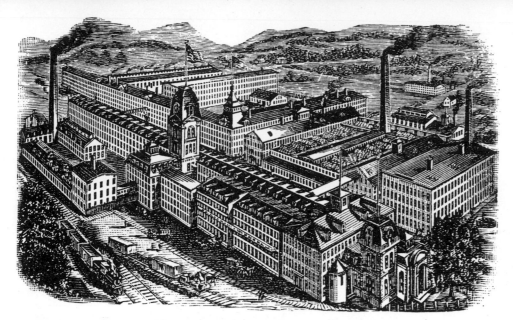

MERIDEN : MERIDEN BRITANNIA CO.

Victorian factories are impressive by sheer size; the long façades with bay after bay are often broken by handsome towers.

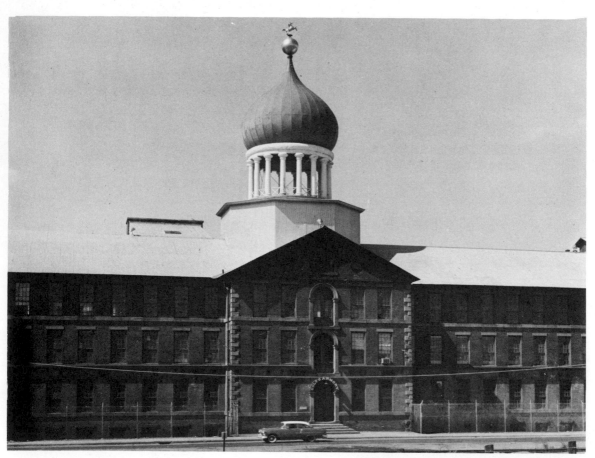

JOHN MAASS

Colt's Armory was built in the forties at Hartford, Connecticut. The oriental-looking dome is topped by the trademark, a golden colt. Colonel Colt's home, Armsmere, also had some architectural touches of the Orient.

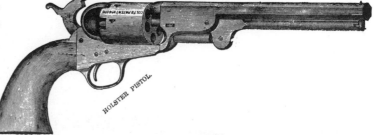

Some specimens of Victorian park and garden architecture:

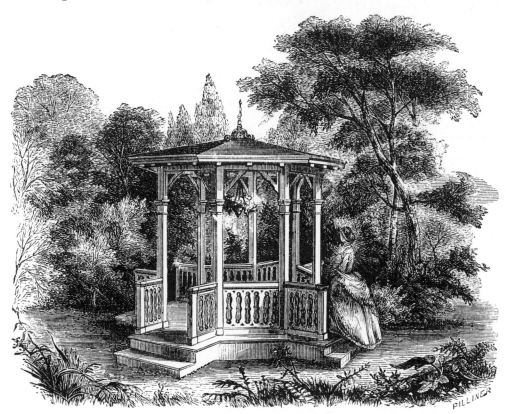

The lady is probably keeping a tryst; the "summerhouse" was a favorite spot for Victorian romance.

Mark Twain's famous octagonal study is supposedly patterned after a riverboat pilot's cabin but looks like most Victorian summerhouses and bandstands. It is now on the campus of Elmira College at Elmira, New York.

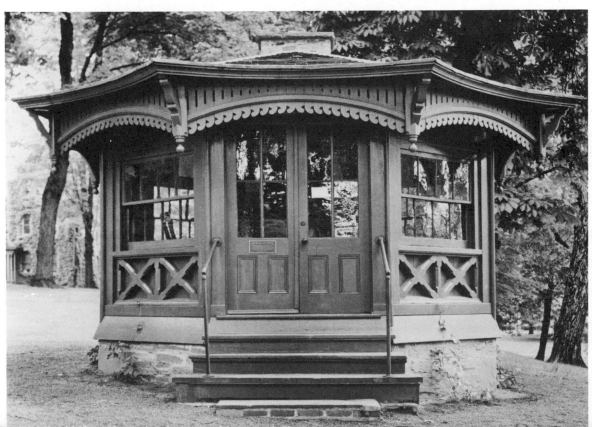

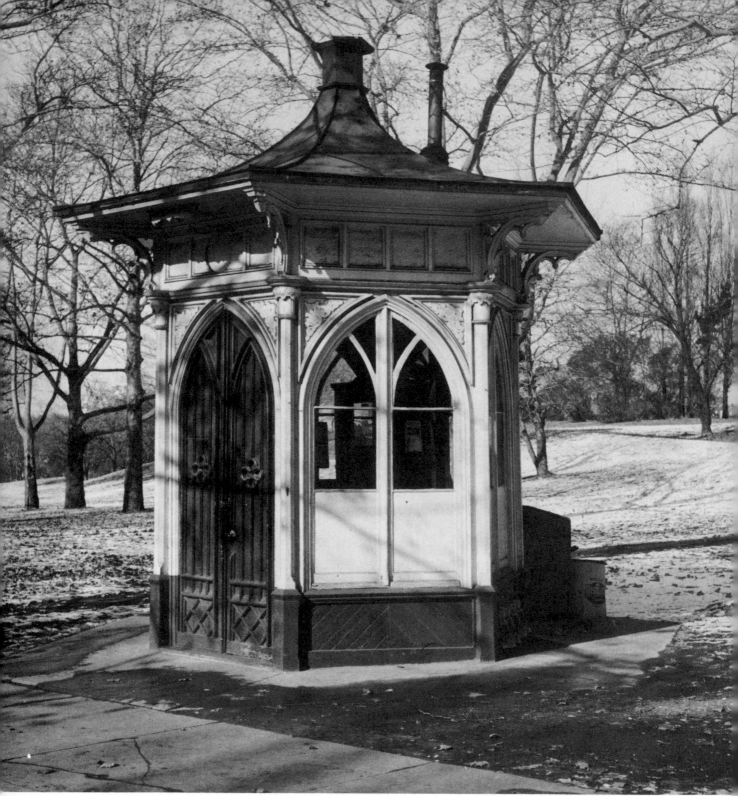

A Carpenter Gothic park guard shelter in Fairmount Park, Philadelphia.

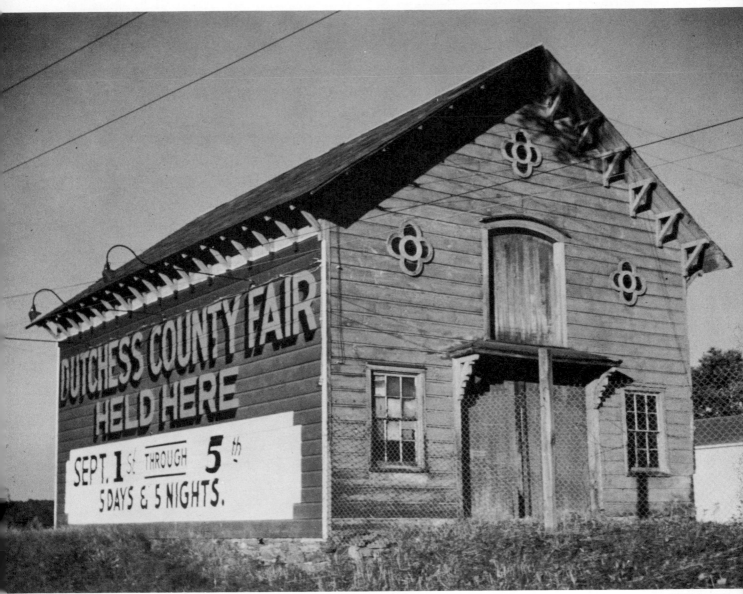

Many fair grounds still have Victorian buildings like "Judges' Pavilions" and "Floral Halls."

163

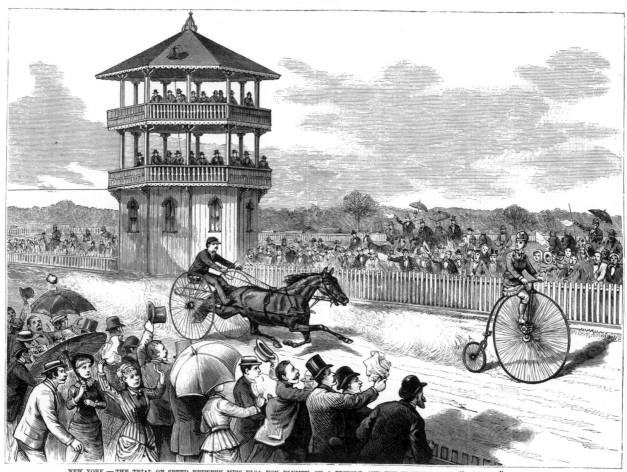

NEW YORK. — THE TRIAL OF SPEED BETWEEN MISS ELSA VON BLUMEN, ON A BICYCLE, AND THE TROTTING MARE "HATTIE R," AT ROCHESTER. FROM A SKETCH BY BURT MILLER. — SEE PAGE 267.

Gingerbread architecture goes to the races.

The clubhouse of the Maryland Jockey Club at Pimlico.

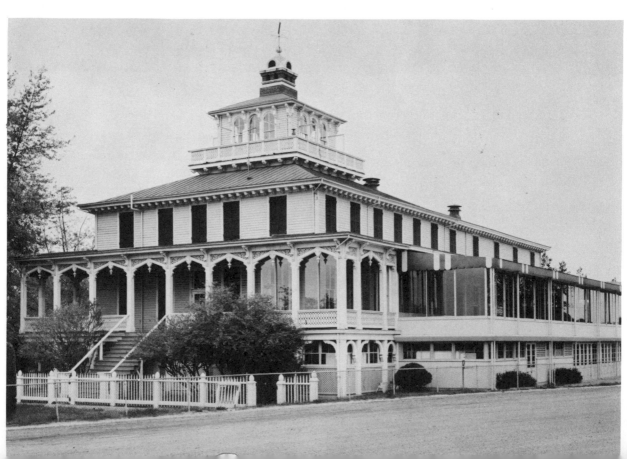

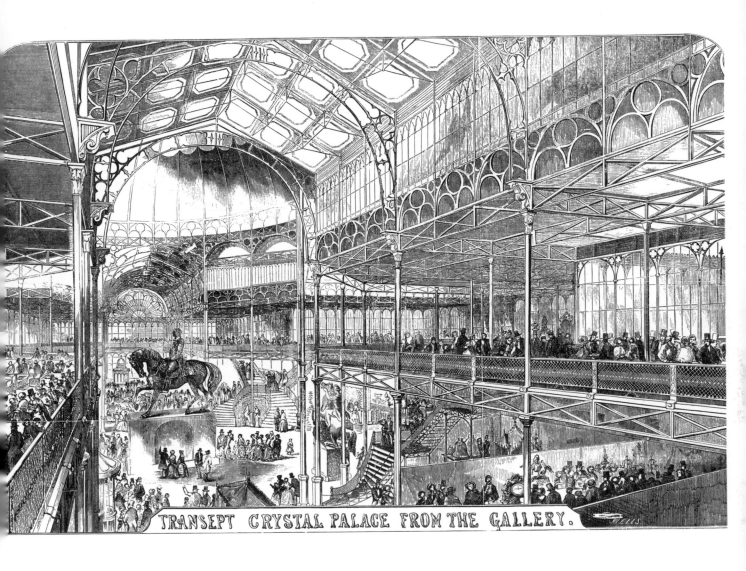

TRANSEPT CRYSTAL PALACE FROM THE GALLERY.

The Victorians invented the World's Fair. The New York "Exhibition of the Industry of all Nations" in 1853 was a private venture imitating the Great London Exhibition of 1851. Even the name "Crystal Palace" was borrowed from the famed London building. The New York Crystal Palace stood on Reservoir Square, now called Bryant Park. The iron and glass structure caught fire in 1858 and was completely destroyed in a quarter of an hour.

165

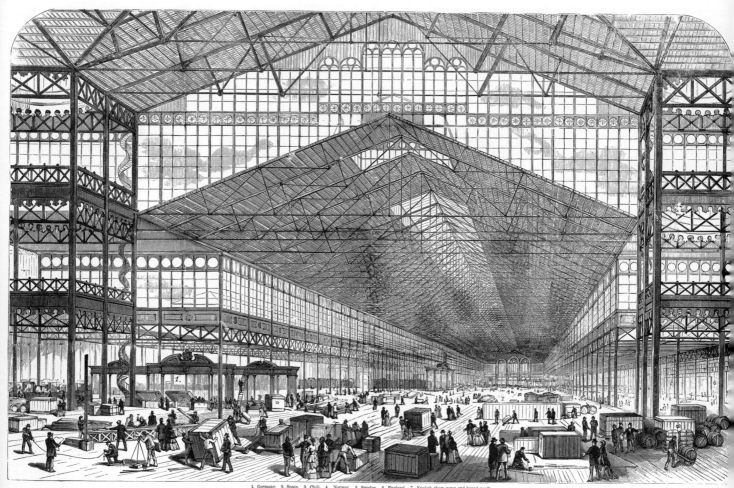

1. Germany. 2. Spain. 3. Chili. 4. Norway. 5. Sweden. 6. England. 7. English show-cases and boxed goods.

INTERIOR OF THE MAIN BUILDING SHOWING THE VARIOUS PAVILIONS AND SHOW-CASES CONSTRUCTED AND IN PROCESS OF ERECTION.

The International Exhibition of 1876 was held in Philadelphia to celebrate the Centennial of American Independence. It was on a gigantic scale, there were over 30,000 exhibitors from 51 countries and nearly ten million visitors passed through the turnstiles between May and November.

The Centennial was a great showcase of Victorianism; the display of scientific and industrial progress was magnificent but the exhibits of fine and decorative arts strike us as monstrosities.

166

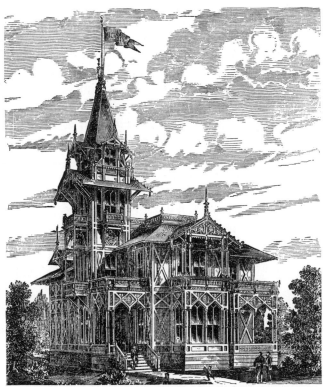

Michigan State Building, Centennial Exposition, Philadelphia.
In the absence of any appropriation from the State, this building was erected mainly through the exertions of the Michigan State Centennial Board and Julius Hess, the architect, at a cost of about $15,000. It is constructed entirely of Michigan lumber, above the foundation. The inside as well as the outside of the building is highly decorative. The walls and ceilings inside the building are panneled, no plastering being used, and the floors of several rooms are inlaid to neat patterns.

The Centennial's temporary architecture was charged with vitality. These beflagged pavilions had a Victorian exuberance which is exactly the right spirit for such a festive event. The state pavilions were picturesque variations of residential buildings, three of them are still standing: The Ohio Building on the original site in Fairmount Park, the Wisconsin Building has been moved to a suburb of Philadelphia, the Maryland House is now in a Baltimore park.

The Statue of Liberty was a Centennial gift from the French Republic and the torch was exhibited at Philadelphia before it went up in New York harbor.

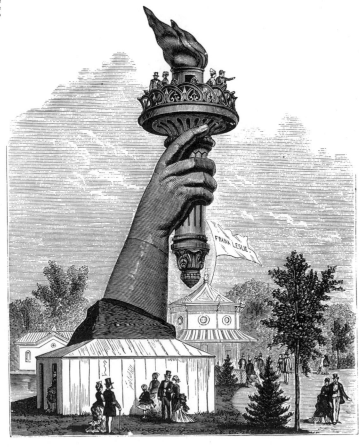

Queen Victoria had nine children which was not uncommon in her time. All of them lived to grow up — few families had such good fortune in a century of dreadful infant mortality. So the Victorians spent a great deal of time visiting graves. There were few public parks until the latter part of the nineteenth century; Victorian cemeteries were beautifully landscaped and designed to be pleasant places for a Sunday walk. Great cemeteries like Brooklyn's Greenwood and Philadelphia's Laurel Hill were celebrated sights for tourists, quite frankly described as "one of the most enchanting spots in this or any country" or "a charming pleasure ground." Victorian cemeteries had pleasing names — Forest Lawn, Cypress Hill, Evergreen, Mount Hope, Harmony Grove — and the tombstones were inscribed with gentle sentiments like "Entered Spirit Life," "Born into Summerland" or "She faltered by the wayside and the angels took her home."

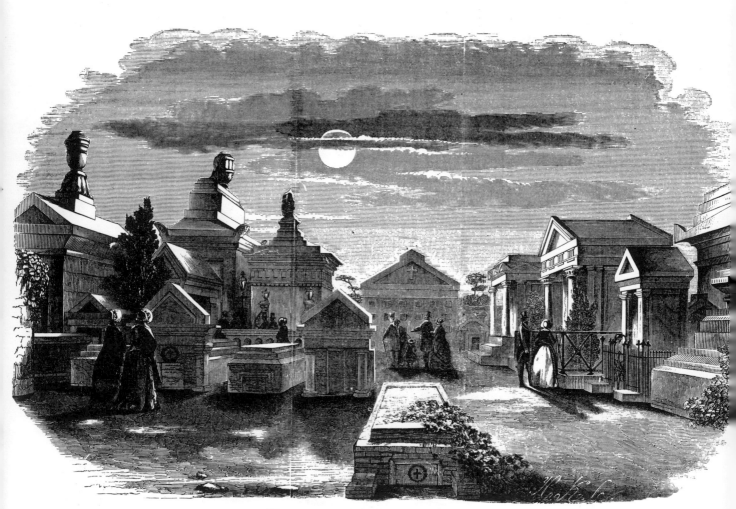

FRENCH CEMETERY, AT NEW ORLEANS, LOUISIANA.

New Orleans' famous cemeteries are unusual; the tombs were built entirely above ground because of the humid soil.

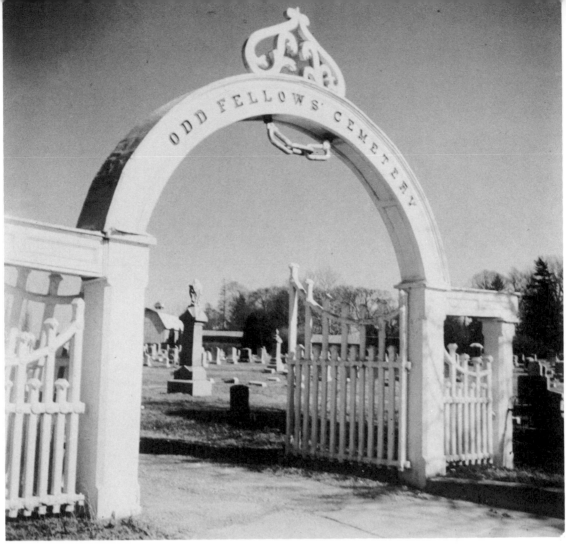

Even small town cemeteries had pretty gates and chapels. Two examples from Delaware at Smyrna and Dover.

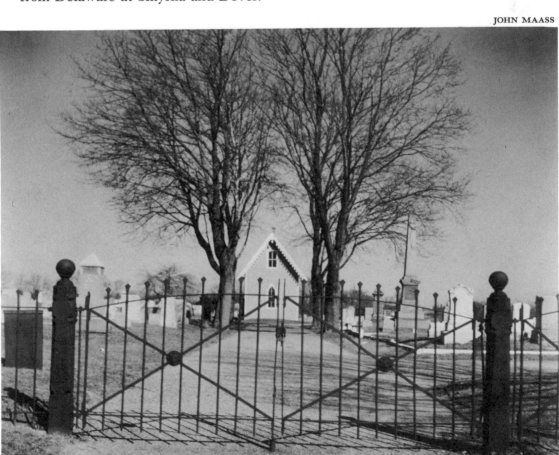

CHAPTER 7

THE REDISCOVERY

*Nothing is so dangerous as being
too modern. One is apt to grow
old-fashioned quite suddenly.*

— OSCAR WILDE

The Victorians adored buildings in a half-ruined state, they called it "pleasing decay." Their own houses sank into this condition of fascinating disrepair after they had become unfashionable.

The centers of gravity in American cities have shifted a great deal since the nineteenth century. Once respectable "downtown" sections often became blighted areas. Stately homes stood empty on their weedy lots or were turned into seedy rooming houses. This is where the cliché of the "gloomy, sinister Victorian mansion" got its start — shuttered houses which have not had a coat of paint in decades naturally assume a mournful look. In popular fiction the Victorian house became a likely background for murder and the preferred haunt of ghosts.

Empty or moldering houses have a peculiar attraction for children and other people with imagination; Victorian houses have inspired a whole gallery of word pictures by American writers. Listen to William Faulkner:

> It was a big, squarish frame house that had once been white, decorated with cupolas and spires and scrolled balconies in the heavily lightsome style of the seventies, set on what had once been our most select street. But garages and cotton gins had encroached and obliterated even the august names of the neighborhood; only Miss Emily's house was left, lifting its stubborn and coquettish decay above the cotton wagons and the gasoline pumps — an eyesore among eyesores.

Look at a Los Angeles neighborhood through the eyes of Raymond Chandler:

> Bunker Hill is old town, lost town, shabby town, crook town. Once, very long ago, it was the choice residential district of the city, and there are still standing a few of the jigsaw Gothic mansions with wide porches and walls covered with round-end shingles and full corner bay windows with spindle turrets. They are all rooming houses now, their parquetry floors are scratched and worn through the once glossy finish and the wide sweeping staircases

173

are dark with time and with cheap varnish laid on over generations of dirt. In the tall rooms haggard landladies bicker with shifty tenants. On the wide cool front porches, reaching their cracked shoes into the sun, and staring at nothing, sit the old men with faces like lost battles.

Or consider this wonderfully aggressive view of Washington by Philip Wylie:

A city filled with every classical incubus of architecture, with a hundred brown boxes of buildings that grow like fungus in the midst of its proudest and most highly marbleized environs, a city without proportion or color or quality, a city from which lurch dingy thoroughfares strewn with staggering edifices that present every sullen, rococo, snarling, sick, noxious and absurd form of vainglorious house and apartment architecture designed in the long decades of Victorian false front and the subsequent age of atrabilious brick to assuage the cheap passions of the middle class and the Middle West.

Here is a rarity, a sympathetic description, by Booth Tarkington:

At the beginning of the Ambersons' great period most of the houses of the Midland town were of a pleasant architecture. They lacked style but also lacked pretentiousness and whatever does not pretend at all has style enough. They stood in commodious yards well shaded by leftover forest trees, elm and walnut and beech with here and there a line of tall sycamores where the land had been made by filling bayous from the creek. The house of a "prominent resident" was built of brick upon a stone foundation or of wood upon a brick foundation. Usually it had a "front porch" and a "back porch," often a "side porch," too. There was a "front hall," there was a "side hall" and sometimes a "back hall." From the "front hall" opened three rooms, the "parlour," the "sitting room" and the "library," and the library could show warrant to its title — for some reason these people bought books. Commonly the family sat more in the library than in the "sitting room," while callers when they came formally, were kept to the "parlour," a place of formidable polish and discomfort. The upholstery of the library furniture was a little shabby, but the hostile chairs

174

and sofa of the "parlour" always looked new. For all the wear and tear they got they should have lasted a thousand years. Upstairs were the bedrooms, "mother-and-father's room," the largest; a smaller room for one or two sons, another for one or two daughters; each of these rooms containing a double bed, a "washstand," a "bureau," a wardrobe, a little table, a rocking chair, and often a chair or two that had been slightly damaged downstairs but not enough to justify either the expense of repair or decisive abandonment in the attic. And there was always a "spare-room" for visitors (where the sewing machine usually was kept) and during the seventies there developed an appreciation of the necessity for a bathroom.

The Victorian house is like a rugged character actor who steals the scene from the smooth-faced leading man; rich in shape, color and texture, it has long been a favorite model for artists and photographers*. In fact, these houses are so highly designed that it is quite difficult to make a really bad picture of such a perfect subject.

Writers and artists began to rediscover Victorian architecture in the nineteen twenties and thirties; the general revival of interest in Victoriana is a post-World War II phenomenon. It was inevitable. The artifacts of the immediate past look merely "dated" but the Victorian era is now beyond the memory of even the oldest living people and has become "history." So a flapper dress is simply ridiculous while the bustle gown has assumed an aura of beauty. The Industrial Revolution had multiplied the number and variety of manufactured objects, the collector of American Victoriana is therefore not limited to such conventional items as silver, glass and china. Every imaginable object of nineteenth century making — toy banks, cigar store Indians, buttons, paperweights, valentines, circus posters, daguerrotype cases, cast-iron lawn deer — is now being ardently collected.

---

* Edward Hopper, Charles Burchfield, Walter Stuempfig, Dong Kingman, Ben Shahn, Saul Steinberg are some of the most distinguished American artists who have been fascinated by Victorian buildings. Walker Evans and the others who made the great documentary record for the Farm Security Administration are outstanding among the photographers.

Victorian furnishings went from the parlor to the attic, from the attic to the junkshop. Within recent years they have moved from the junkshop to the Antique Shoppe and from the Antique Shoppe back into the parlor. That keen observer of American customs, Mr. Russell Lynes, noted early that the highbrows were buying Victorian bric-a-brac. The lowbrows had of course always been sure that heavy, old-fashioned furniture was just fine. Between those two groups — who know what they like — bulks the middle class which relies on the advice of syndicated experts in such matters as love, marriage, etiquette and interior decoration. These oracles used to tell the public that everything Victorian was "in bad taste" but they sharply reversed themselves in the nineteen fifties. The following advertisement which appeared in 1956 tells the story:

Just what the decorator ordered:

VICTORIAN CHAIRS

Just what the Budget needed:

SALE $49.95

Usually $79.95 and $87.95

Well of course you have fallen for Victorian. What has more charm? What has more elegance? What else could you put in that corner of the living room? And Gimbel's has made a tremendous purchase . . . over 18 styles . . . beautiful reproductions.

Reproductions of Victorian furniture are now being mass-produced* but we are not likely to see any Neo-Victorian houses built.

Nineteenth century "primitive" American art has become both a critical and a box-office success and American vernacular architecture deserves equal attention. Everyone — in every part of the country — can still be a discoverer in this field. But the building you find today may be gone tomorrow; anyone proposing to tamper with the most

---

* Including aluminum replicas of cast-iron Victorian furniture.

insignificant colonial house would be branded a Benedict Arnold by the local Historical Society and Women's Club. This loyalty to the eighteenth century is no doubt reinforced by the fact that colonial buildings make profitable tourist attractions. Victorian buildings have few defenders; on the contrary, it is considered a mark of civic virtue and rectitude to tear them down one and all.

Interesting Victorian buildings may be found anywhere — in the city, the suburb, the town, the village, the countryside, just off Main Street or right on it. I spied the back of this promising house from a turnpike; I had to drive thirty miles, on to the nearest exit and back over side roads, before I could look at the front.

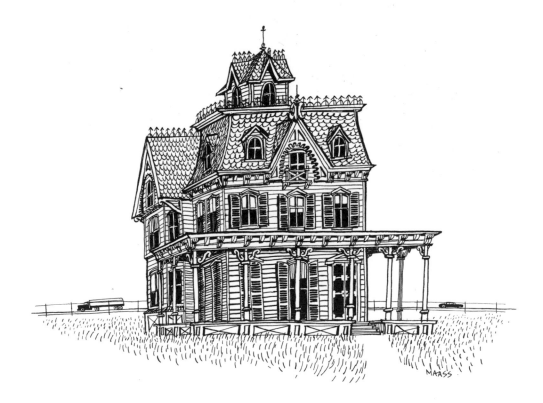

Most owners of Victorian houses seem to like their homes but are apologetic about them because they have been told by self-appointed experts that these houses are "bad architecture." My favorite was the lady who lived in this apparition. When I asked her whether she could tell me anything about its history, she replied, "I am afraid not. You can see for yourself, it's a very ordinary sort of place."

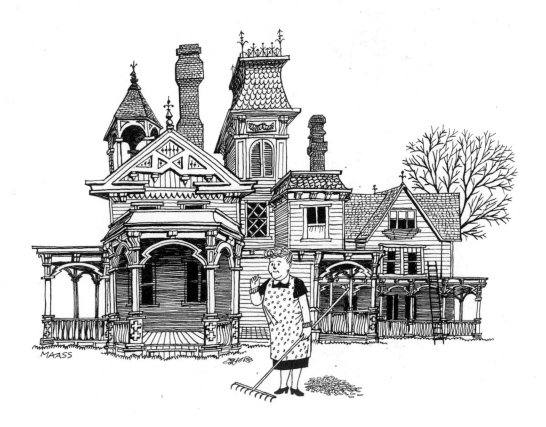

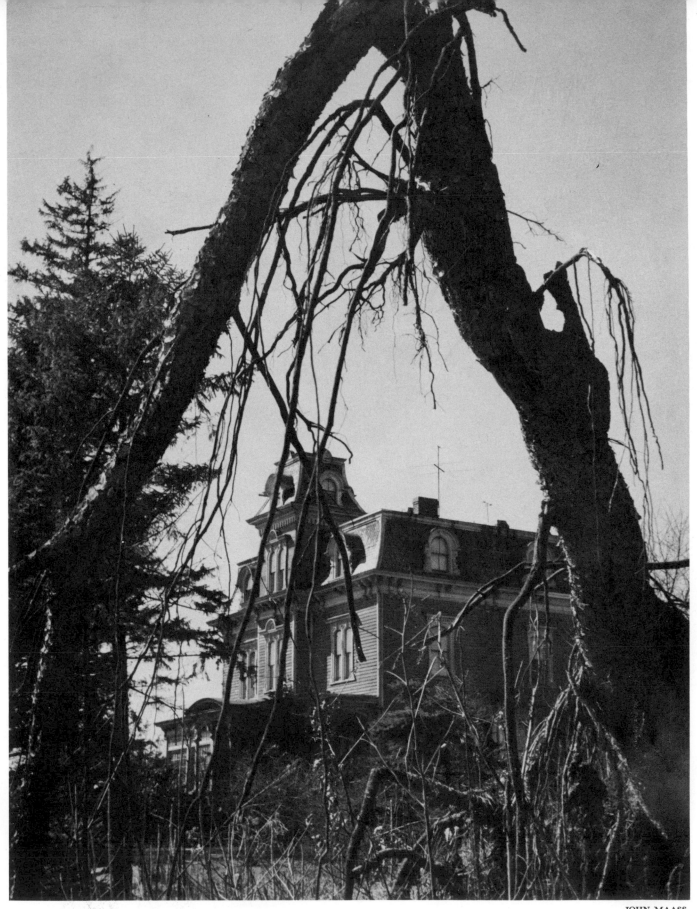

The classic, sinister Victorian mansion — actually a well-kept home at Rockaway, New Jersey.

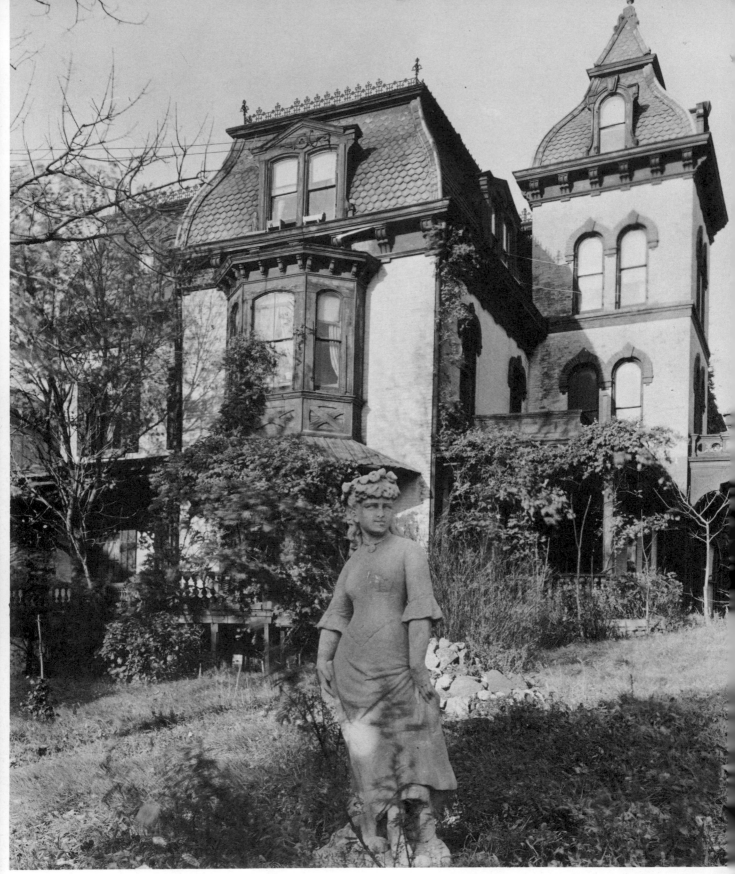

The William Wheelock House was one of the last Victorian survivors in Manhattan.

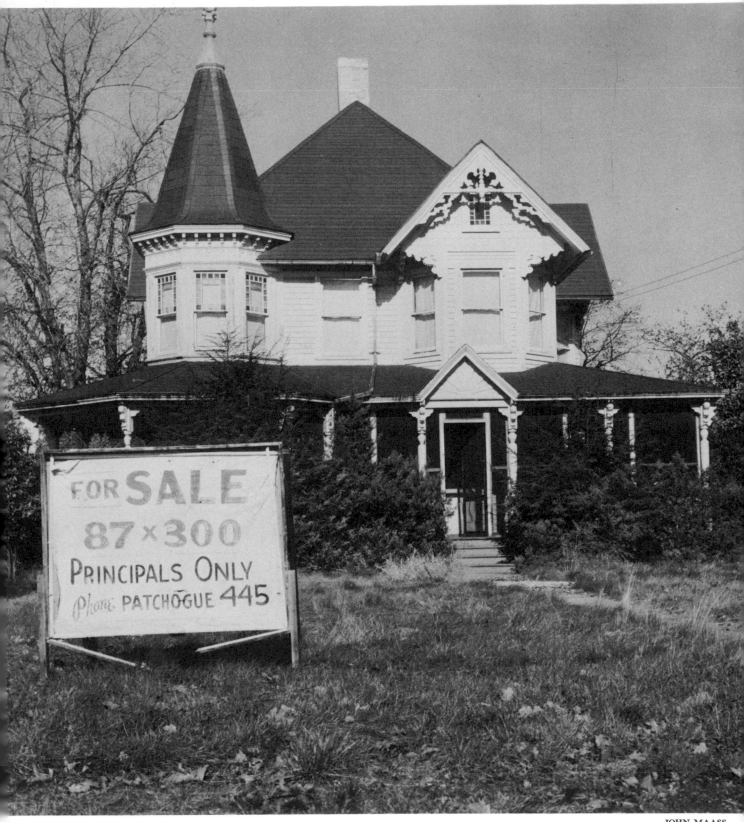

Late Gothic or early "Queen Anne" in Suffolk County, Long Island, N.Y.

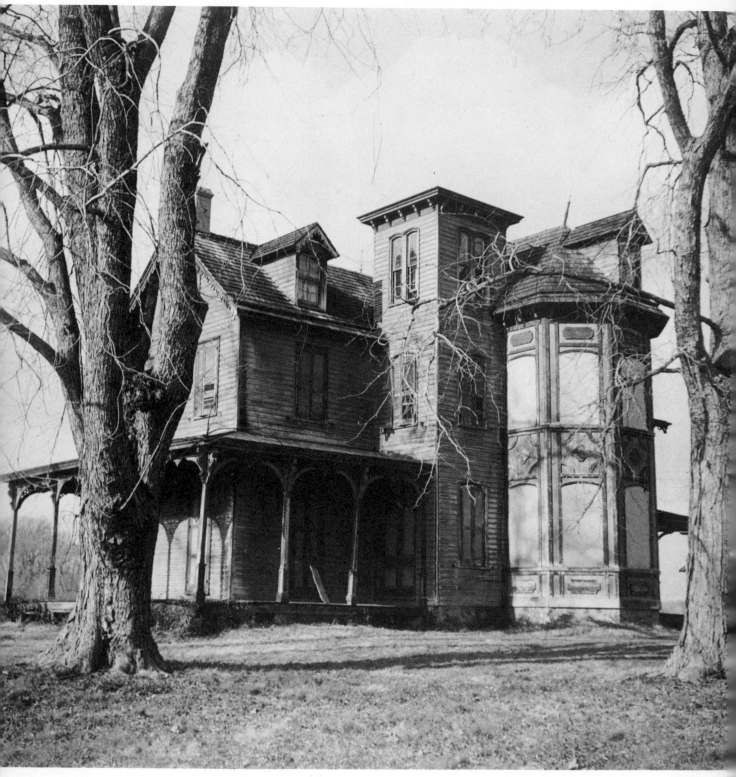

An empty house of striking design at Greenville, Delaware.

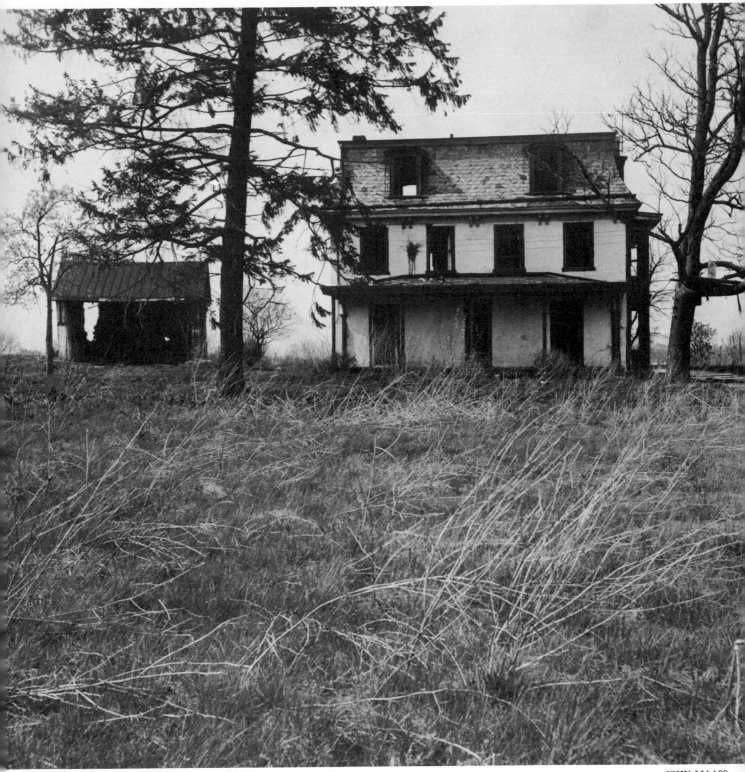

Abandoned farmhouse at King of Prussia, Pennsylvania.

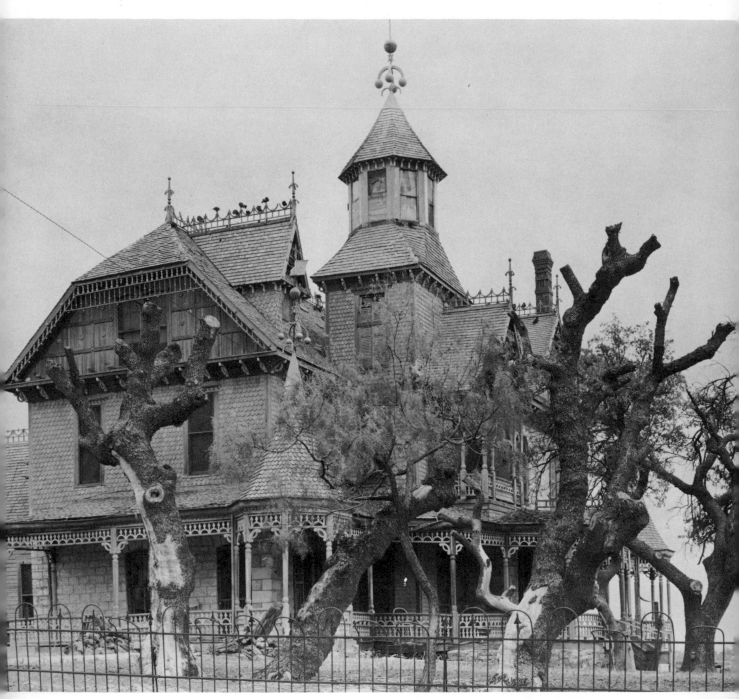

A strange mansion at Comanche, Texas. Note the originality of the fantastic wood- and ironwork from the fence to the top of the tower.

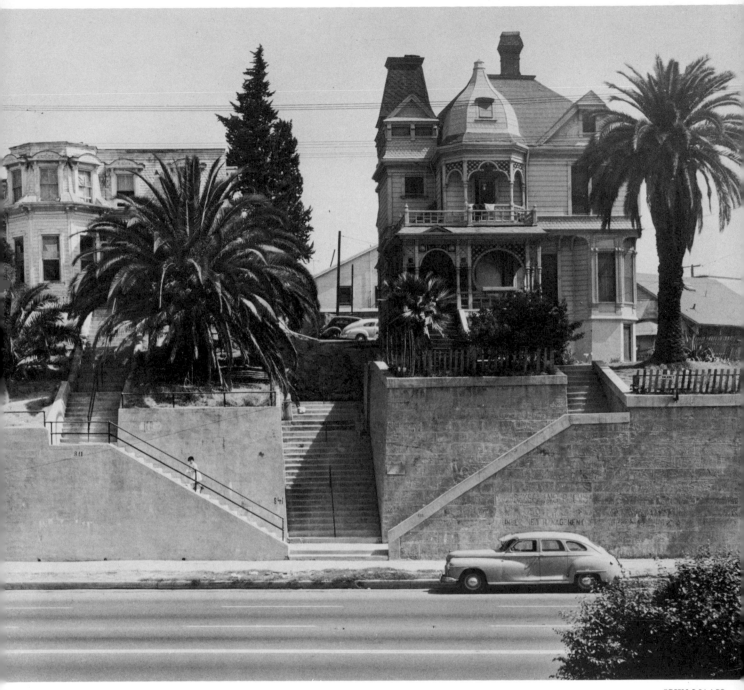

These mansions are now rooming houses on the unfashionable end of Sunset Boulevard, Los Angeles.

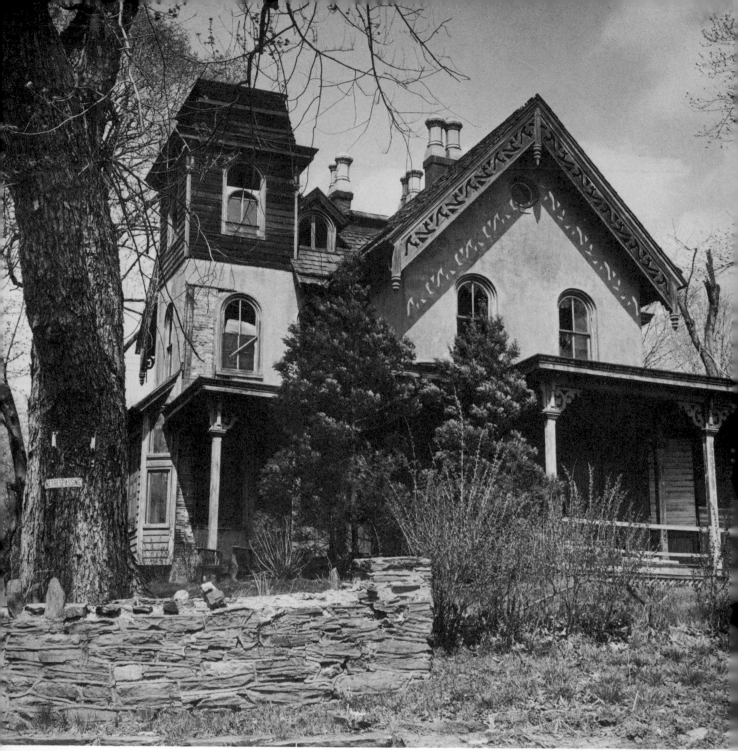

The last owner of this Miquon, Pennsylvania, house collected autos; a dozen rusty hulks still stand in the yard.

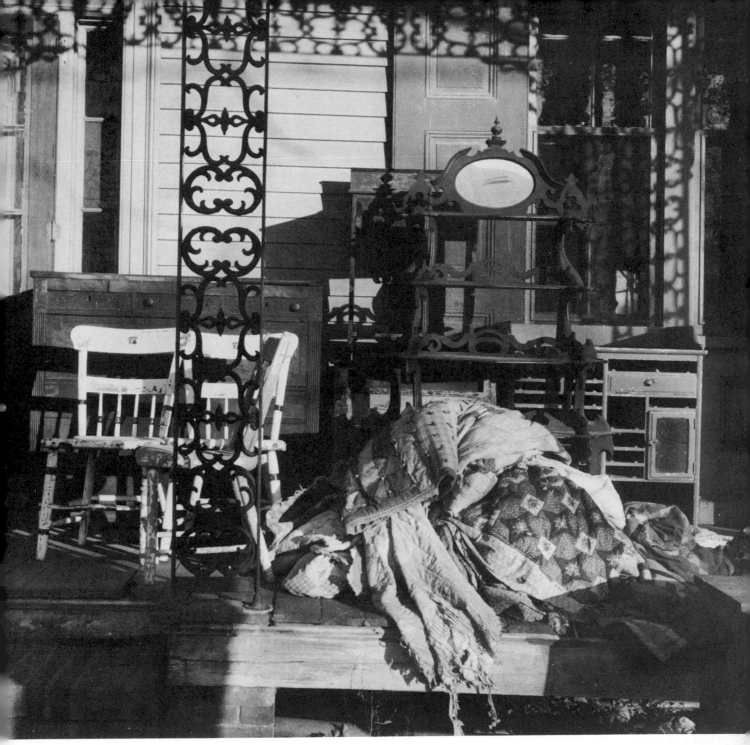

Common Victorian furnishings are now sold in little country antique shops.
Note how the curves on the "whatnot" resemble the cast-iron porch.

187

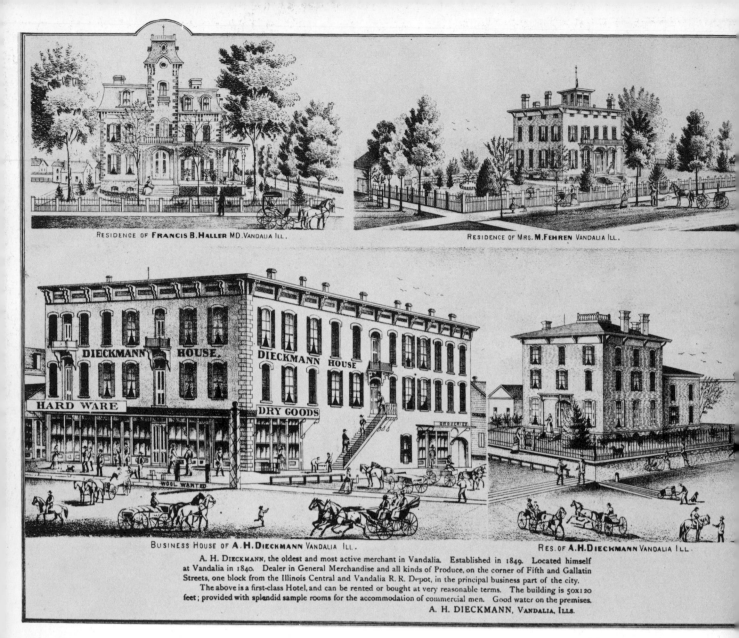

RESIDENCE OF **FRANCIS B. HALLER** MD. VANDALIA ILL.

RESIDENCE OF MRS. **M. FEHREN** VANDALIA ILL.

DIECKMANN HOUSE.

DIECKMANN HOUSE

HARD WARE

DRY GOODS

GROCERIES

WOOL WANTED

BUSINESS HOUSE OF **A. H. DIECKMANN** VANDALIA ILL.

RES. OF **A. H. DIECKMANN** VANDALIA ILL.

A. H. DIECKMANN, the oldest and most active merchant in Vandalia. Established in 1849. Located himself at Vandalia in 1840. Dealer in General Merchandise and all kinds of Produce, on the corner of Fifth and Gallatin Streets, one block from the Illinois Central and Vandalia R. R. Depot, in the principal business part of the city.

The above is a first-class Hotel, and can be rented or bought at very reasonable terms. The building is 50x120 feet; provided with splendid sample rooms for the accommodation of commercial men. Good water on the premises.

A. H. DIECKMANN, VANDALIA, ILLS.

WARNER & BEERS ATLAS OF ILLINOIS, (18

The nineteenth century state and county atlases contained large scale township maps. The publishers would also immortalize substantial citizens — for a fee, they included their biography, portrait and pictures of their home or place of business. The artists often seemed to have trouble with perspective but they made up for it by the lovingly drawn details and the lively sketches of people, horses, cattle, dogs, wagons, buggies and railroad trains. These lithographs are both a documentary record of nineteenth century life and delightful specimens of American folk art. Two more examples of county atlas art are on Pages 142 and 157.

188

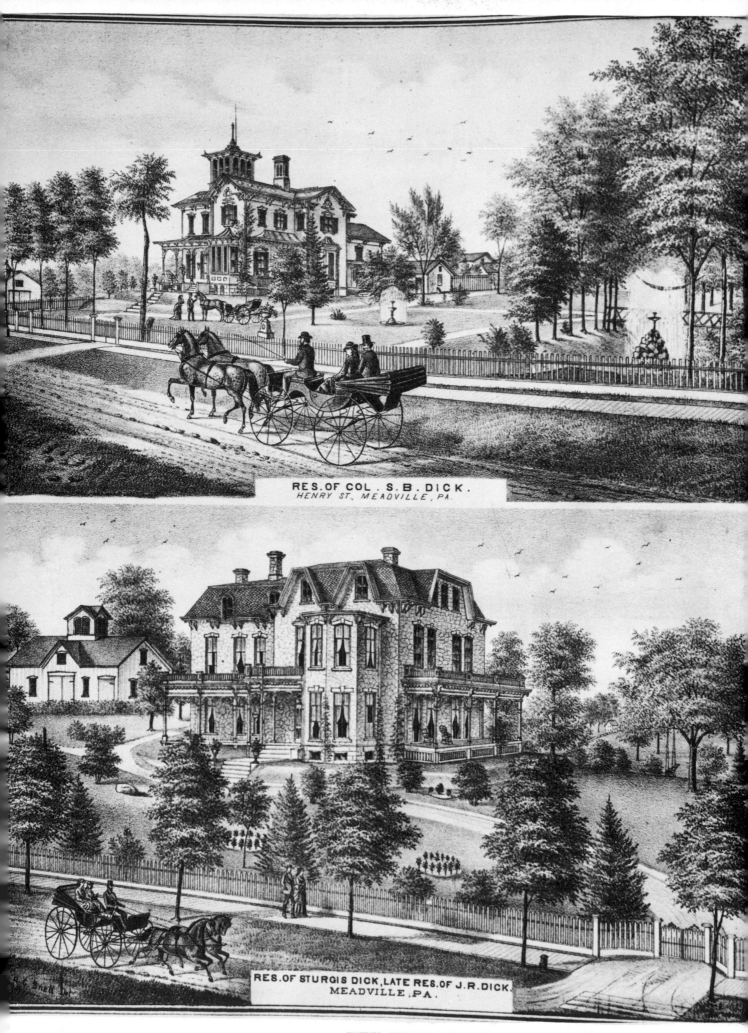

RES. OF COL. S.B. DICK.
HENRY ST. MEADVILLE, PA.

RES. OF STURGIS DICK, LATE RES. OF J.R. DICK.
MEADVILLE, PA.

EVERTS, ENSIGN & EVERTS ATLAS OF CRAWFORD COUNTY, PENNSYLVANIA (1876)

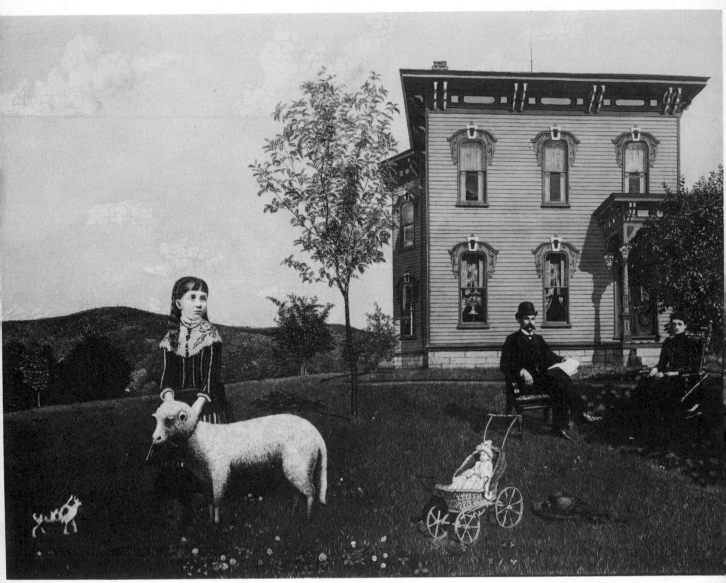

Edwin Romanzo Elmer (what a name!) was an inventor and recently re-discovered artist of Ashfield, Massachusetts. When his little daughter died, he painted her with the lamb in this haunting "mourning picture." The Elmers and their home are in the background.

190

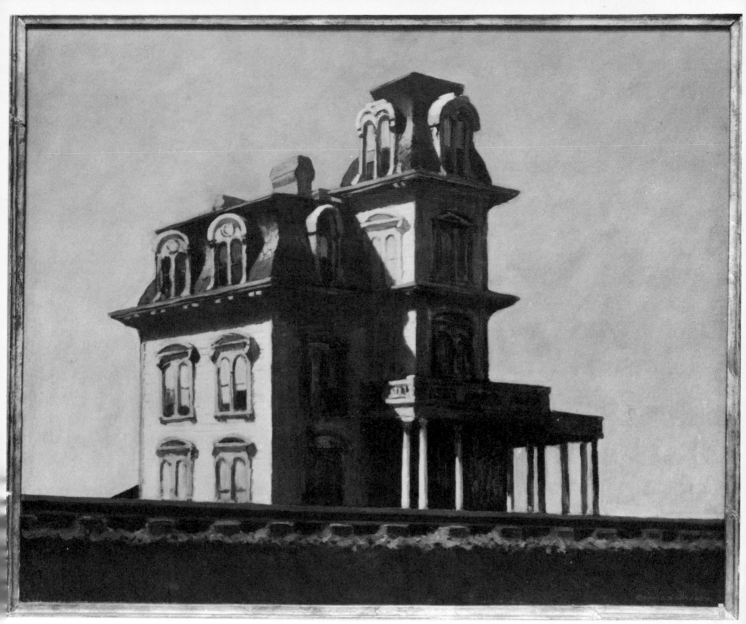

Edward Hopper's famous "House by the Railroad" (1925) looks so real, it is surprising to learn that "he painted it out of his head." There are some similar houses near the Erie Railroad tracks in Hopper's native Rockland County, New York.

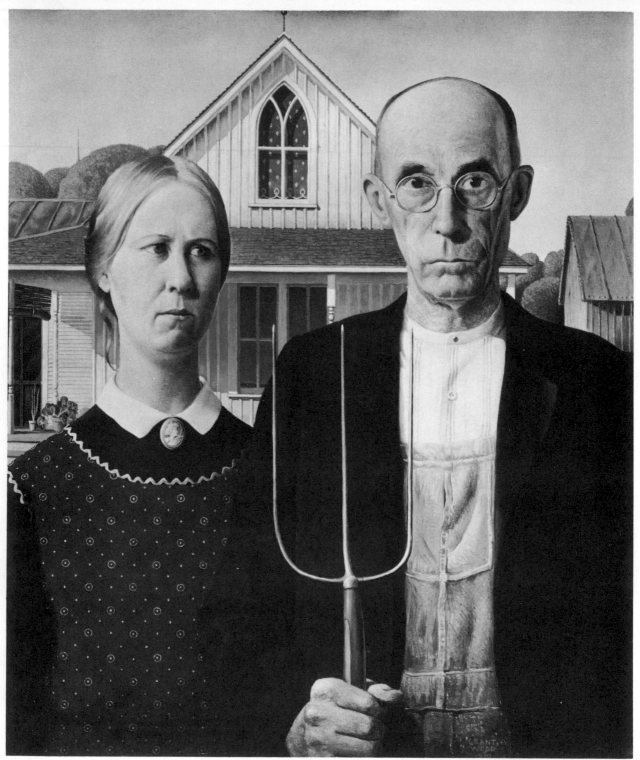

Grand Wood's "American Gothic" created a sensation when it was first exhibited in 1930. The models are the artist's sister and his dentist. The house stands in Eldon, Iowa.

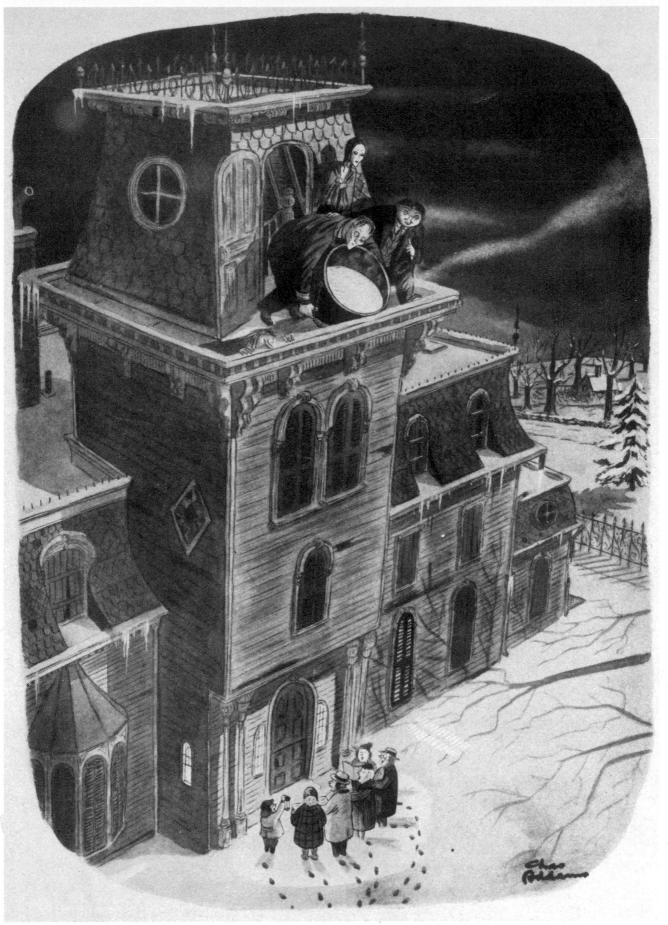

Charles Addams has tenanted the Victorian mansion with fiends but it is obvious that he loves those houses.

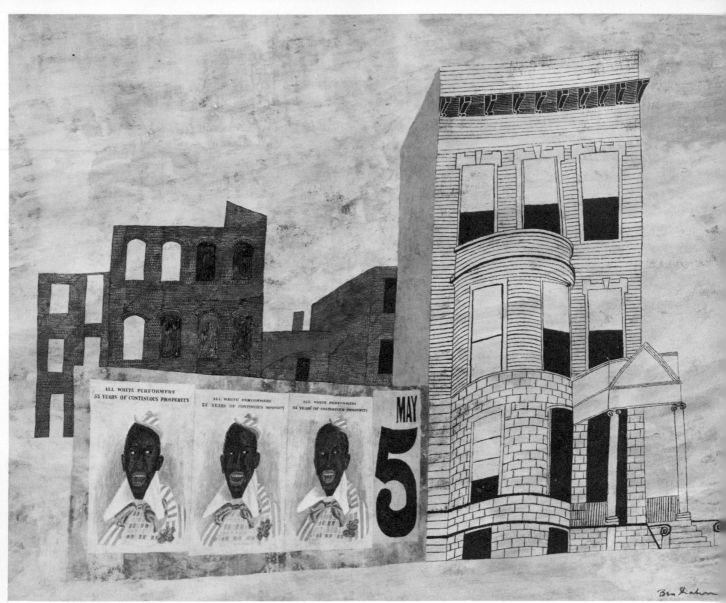

The humanist artist Ben Shahn has long been interested in American popular architecture. His paintings and drawings on this subject combine great formal beauty with a searching, documentary quality. The artist's father was a gingerbread carver in Russia.

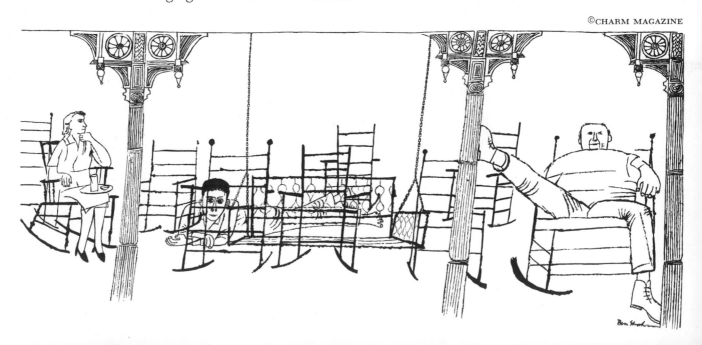

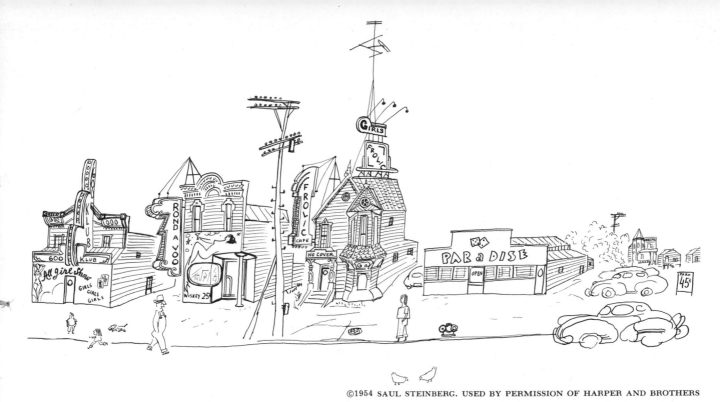

Saul Steinberg was trained as an architect and came to the United States as a mature man. His uncanny, penetrating vision of America was never blunted by contemptuous familiarity.

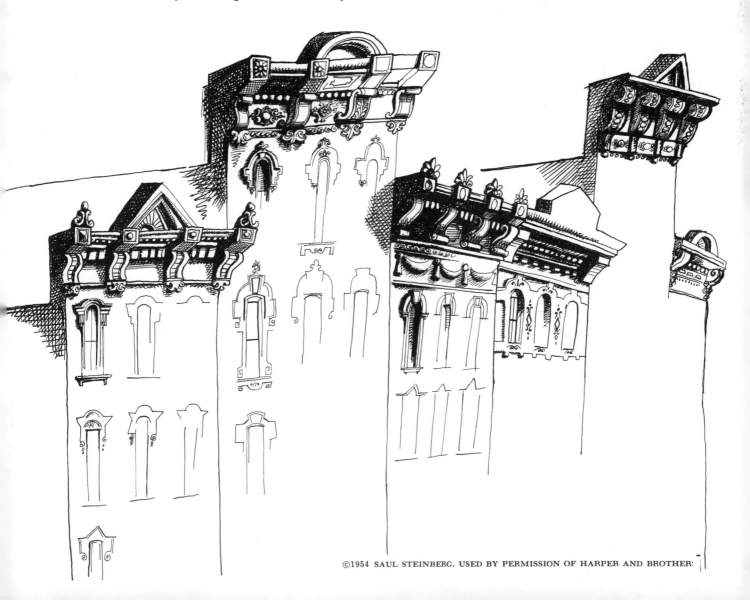

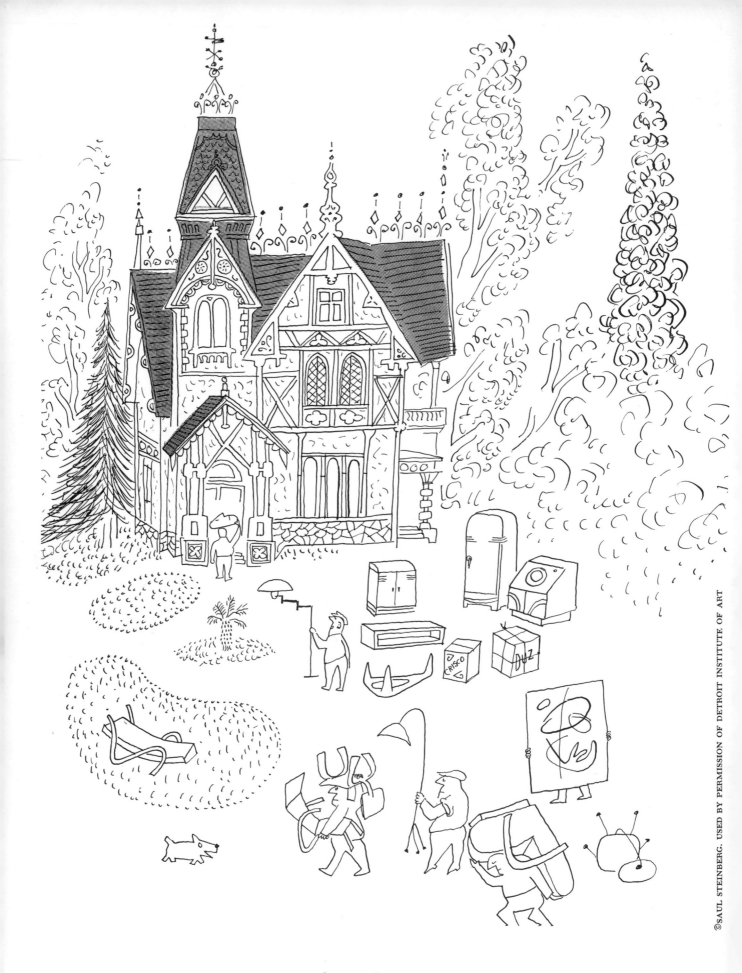

This is The End

A Note on The Pictures

The Victorian illustrations in this book are from the author's collection of nineteenth century records. Architectural pattern books are a prime source of pictures; a wealth of graphic material on buildings is found in non-architectural books such as state and county atlases, local histories, city directories, guides and catalogs. Architecture was considered newsworthy and excellent engravings were presented by general periodicals like *Gleason's Pictorial Drawing-Room Companion, Ballou's Pictorial Drawing-Room Companion, Harper's New Monthly Magazine, Putnams Monthly Magazine, Harper's Weekly, Frank Leslie's Illustrated Newspaper, Harper's Bazaar* and *Godey's Lady's Book.*

The period discussed in this book was the golden age of wood engraving. Drawings, paintings and photographs were reproduced in books and periodicals through the wood engraver's skill. This craft demanded exacting discipline and design ability of a very high order. Look closely at these marvels of craftsmanship: Every black line you see — and there are thousands of lines in a fair-sized illustration — is the impression of a little ridge of wood which was left standing after the engraver cut away the surface of a boxwood block all around it. The technique was highly standardized: when a large illustration had to be engraved in a hurry to make the deadline, the work would be divided among several engravers. Only a thin white line shows where their small blocks were joined to form one large wood engraving.

In the eighteen eighties the inventions of process engraving and the halftone screen displaced wood engraving as a medium of reproduction. Aldous Huxley has pointed out the result — the photographic camera took over the jobs of the skilled craftsmen who had made beautiful reproductions of first-rate art; they were then left free to produce second-rate art of their own.

197

Selected Bibliography

History, technology, economics, social life, literature, art, fashion — all have important bearing on architecture. A full bibliography of nineteenth century sources would have to contain thousands of titles. This brief list has therefore been limited to books about buildings and closely related subjects which are accessible to the general reader. Biographies, articles and pamphlets are not included. The dates given are those of the first edition.

General

ANDREWS, WAYNE; *Architecture, Ambition and Americans.*
New York, Harper and Brothers, 1955.
Highly personal History.

BARMAN, CHRISTIAN; *An Introduction to Railway Architecture.*
London, Art and Technics, 1950.
A masterly British study.

CASSON, HUGH; *An Introduction to Victorian Architecture.*
London, Art and Technics, 1948.
A brilliant gem from Britain.

EVANS, WALKER; *American Photographs.*
New York, Museum of Modern Art, 1938.
By the rediscoverer of American Victorian architecture.

GIEDION, SIGFRIED; *Time, Space and Architecture,* The Growth of a New Tradition.
Cambridge, Harvard University Press, 1941.

GIEDION, SIGFRIED; *Mechanization Takes Command,* A Contribution to Anonymous History.
New York, Oxford University Press, 1948.
Both are packed with creative research and fascinating illustrations.

HAMLIN, TALBOT F.; *Greek Revival Architecture in America.*
New York, Oxford University Press, 1944.
The standard work.

HITCHCOCK, HENRY-RUSSELL; *Early Victorian Architecture in Britain.*
New Haven, Yale University Press, 1954.
Monumental work by an American scholar.

JONES, BARBARA; *The Unsophisticated Arts.*
London, Architectural Press, 1951.
Delightful book on British popular design, including much Victoriana.

KOUWENHOWEN, JOHN A.; *Made in America,* The Arts in Modern Civilization.
Garden City, Doubleday and Company, 1948.
The pioneer book on vernacular design.

LARKIN, OLIVER W.; *Art and Life in America*
New York, Rinehart and Company, 1950.
An ambitious and successful attempt to present all visual arts in a single volume.

LICHTEN, FRANCES; *Decorative Arts of Victoria's Era.*
New York, Charles Scribner's Sons, 1950.
Most understanding of Victorian people.

LYNES, RUSSELL; *The Tastemakers.*
New York, Harper and Brothers, 1954.
By the urbane editor of "Harper's Magazine."

MEEKS, CARROLL L. V.; *The Railroad Station,* An Architectural History.
New Haven, Yale University Press, 1956.
Authoritative study covering both Europe and America.

SELECTED BIBLIOGRAPHY

MORRISON, HUGH; *Early American Architecture*, From the First Colonial Settlements to the National Period.
New York, Oxford University Press, 1952.
The standard history.

MUMFORD, LEWIS; *Sticks and Stones*, A Study of American Architecture and Civilization.
New York, Horace Liveright, 1924.

MUMFORD, LEWIS; *The Brown Decades*, A Study of the Arts in America 1865-1895.
New York, Harcourt, Brace and Company, 1931.
Two works of genius.

PEVSNER, NIKOLAUS; *High Victorian Design*, A Study of the Exhibits of 1851.
London, Architectural Press, 1951.
Keen analysis by a famous art historian.

PICKERING, ERNEST; *The Homes of America*.
New York, Thomas Y. Crowell Company, 1951.
Good popular history.

PIPER, JOHN; *Buildings and Prospects*.
London, Architectural Press, 1948.
Perceptive essays by a British artist.

SCULLY, VINCENT J.; *The Shingle Style*, Architectural Theory and Design from Richardson to the origins of Wright.
New Haven, Yale University Press, 1955.
A doctoral dissertation.

Regional and Local

ABBOTT, BERENICE; *Changing New York*.
New York, E. P. Dutton and Company, 1939.

BOWEN, CROSWELL; *Great River of the Mountains: The Hudson*.
New York, Hastings House, 1941.

CARMER, CARL; *The Hudson.*
New York, Farrar and Rinehart, 1939.

COOLIDGE, JOHN P.; *Mill and Mansion,* A Study of Architecture and Society
in Lowell, Massachusetts, 1820-1865.
New York, Columbia University Press, 1942.

DICKSON, HAROLD E.; *A Hundred Pennsylvania Buildings.*
State College, Penn., Bald Eagle Press, 1954.

DOWNING, ANTOINETTE AND SCULLY, VINCENT J.; *The Architectural Heritage
of Newport, Rhode Island.*
Cambridge, Harvard University Press, 1952.

DRURY, JOHN; *Old Chicago Houses.*
Chicago, University of Chicago Press, 1941.

DRURY, JOHN; *Historic Midwest Houses.*
Minneapolis, University of Minnesota Press, 1947.

DRURY, JOHN; *Old Illinois Houses.*
Springfield, Illinois State Historical Society, 1948.

HITCHCOCK, HENRY-RUSSELL; *Rhode Island Architecture.*
Providence, Rhode Island Museum Press, 1939.

HOWLAND, RICHARD HUBBARD AND SPENCER, ELEANOR PATTERSON; *The Architecture of Baltimore,* A Pictorial History.
Baltimore, Johns Hopkins Press, 1953.

KILHAM, WALTER H.; *Boston After Bulfinch,* An Account of its Architecture
1800-1900.
Cambridge, Harvard University Press, 1946.

KOUWENHOVEN, JOHN A.; The Columbia Historical Portrait of New York.
Garden City, Doubleday & Company, Inc., 1953.

LAUGHLIN, CLARENCE JOHN; *Ghosts Along The Mississippi.*
New York, Charles Scribner's Sons, 1948.

SELECTED BIBLIOGRAPHY

LEWIS, OSCAR; *Here Lived The Californians.*
New York, Rinehart and Company, 1957.

NEWCOMB, REXFORD; *Architecture of the Old Northwest Territory.*
Chicago, University of Chicago Press, 1950.

NEWCOMB, REXFORD; *Architecture in Old Kentucky.*
Urbana, University of Illinois Press, 1953.

WHITE, THEO. B. (Ed.); *Philadelphia Architecture in the Nineteenth Century.*
Philadelphia, University of Pennsylvania Press, 1953.

WOLLE, MURIEL SIBELL; *Stampede to Timberline*, The Ghost Towns and Mining Camps of Colorado.
Boulder, Muriel S. Wolle, 1949.

WOLLE, MURIEL SIBELL; *The Bonanza Trail,* Ghost Towns and Mining Camps of the West.
Bloomington, University of Indiana Press, 1953.

ADDENDA TO BIBLIOGRAPHY

ANDREWS, WAYNE; *Architecture in America.*
New York, Atheneum Publishers, 1960.

BURCHARD, JOHN and BUSH-BROWN, ALBERT; *The Architecture of America.*
Boston, Little Brown & Co., 1961.

COMSTOCK, HELEN; *American Furniture.*
New York, Viking Press, 1962.

CONDIT, CARL W.; *American Building Art—The Nineteenth Century.*
New York, Oxford Univ. Press, 1960.

GLOAG, JOHN; *Victorian Comfort.*
New York, Macmillan, 1961.

GLOAG, JOHN; *Victorian Taste.*
New York, Macmillan, 1962.

GOWANS, ALAN; *Looking at Architecture in Canada*.
New York, Oxford Univ. Press, 1959.

GOWANS, ALAN; *Images of American Living*.
Philadelphia, J. B. Lippincott Co., 1963.

HITCHCOCK, HENRY-RUSSELL; *Architecture: Nineteenth & Twentieth Centuries*.
Baltimore, Penguin Books, 1958.

KIRKER, HAROLD; *California's Architectural Frontier*.
San Marino, Huntington Library, 1960.

LANCASTER, CLAY; *Architectural Follies in America*.
Rutland, Charles E. Tuttle Co., 1960.

REED, JOHN; *The Hudson Valley*.
New York, Clarkson N. Potter, 1960.

SCHMIDT, CARL F.; *The Octagon Fad*.
Scottsville, Carl F. Schmidt, 1958.

TATUM, GEORGE B.; *Penn's Great Town*.
Philadelphia, Univ. of Pennsylvania Press, 1961.

WEBB, TODD; *Gold Strikes and Ghost Towns*.
Garden City, Doubleday, 1961.

WHITEHILL, WALTER MUIR; *Boston—A Topographical History*.
Cambridge, Harvard Univ. Press, 1959.

Acknowledgments

As an amateur fancier of architecture I am greatly indebted to the scholars who have worked in this field; the lucid writings of Dr. Sigfried Giedion and Sir Hugh Casson were especially stimulating for me.

I would like to thank Dorothy A. Babbs, Edward H. Dare, John Drury, Mrs. Edward Hopper, Grace M. Mayer, Vincent A. R. Primavera and Franklin C. Wood for information which they kindly gave me.

I am most grateful to the artists and photographers who permitted me to reproduce some of their distinguished work: Herbert Bayer, Carl Carmer, Henri Cartier-Bresson, Charles T. Coiner, Erich Hartmann, Fred Lyon, Phillip March, Paul J. Mitarachi, Cas Oorthuys, William Rapp, Walter Reinsel, Selden Rodman, Ben Shahn, Saul Steinberg.

My thanks to the many institutions and organizations which contributed illustrations to this book: *Charm Magazine*, The Chicago Art Institute, The Church of Jesus Christ of Latter Day Saints, Contact Publishing Company, Amsterdam, The Detroit Institute of Arts, Elmira College, Eureka Chamber of Commerce, The Franklin D. Roosevelt Library, Harper & Bros., Illinois Department of Parks, *Industrial Design Magazine*, The Kansas City *Star*, The Library of Congress, Louisiana Department of Commerce, Magnum Photos, Inc., Maine Development Commission, Maryland Jockey Club, Missouri Historical Society, The Museum of Modern Art, The Museum of the City of New York, *The New Yorker Magazine*, The Parish of Trinity Church, Smith College Museum of Art, The University of Tampa, West Virginia University.

Index

207

INDEX

INDEX

209

INDEX

INDEX

INDEX